IS IT "JUST A PHASE"—OR IS SOMETHING REALLY WRONG?

When a child temporarily acts up, parents can identify the immediate problem and respond without judging their child. They deal with the incident without feeling that their child is hopeless, or has a bad attitude. They remember the real child behind the chaos of the moment. But a behavioral disorder is not temporary and does not pass after a good night's sleep. Its persistence makes it far harder to see the child behind the problem.

None of us wants to learn that there is anything seriously wrong with our children. Each one of them is so important, so full of promise, that most parents resist the notion of trouble. But when the truth sets in, when we see that a child is behaviorally disordered, we have begun to overcome the secret handicap.

WHEN ACTING OUT ISN'T ACTING

Understanding Attention-deficit
Hyperactivity and Conduct Disorders
in Children and Adolescents

**by
Lynne W. Weisberg, M.D., Ph.D.
and
Rosalie Greenberg, M.D.**

BANTAM BOOKS
NEW YORK · TORONTO · LONDON · SYDNEY · AUCKLAND

WHEN ACTING OUT ISN'T ACTING

*A Bantam Book / published by arrangement with
The PIA Press*

PRINTING HISTORY
PIA Press edition published 1988
Bantam edition / August 1991

*BANTAM NONFICTION and the portrayal of a boxed "b" are
trademarks of Bantam Books, a division of Bantam Doubleday
Dell Publishing Group, Inc.*

ISBN 0-553-29210-2

Published simultaneously in the United States and Canada

*Bantam Books are published by Bantam Books, a division of
Bantam Doubleday Dell Publishing Group, Inc. Its trademark,
consisting of the words "Bantam Books" and the portrayal of a
rooster, is Registered in U.S. Patent and Trademark Office and in
other countries. Marca Registrada. Bantam Books, 666 Fifth
Avenue, New York, New York 10103.*

PRINTED IN THE UNITED STATES OF AMERICA

OPM   0 9 8 7 6 5 4 3 2 1

This book is not intended to replace personal medical care and supervision; there is no substitute for the experience and information that a doctor can provide. Rather, it is our hope that this book will provide additional information to help people understand the proper use of medication in biopsychiatry.

Proper medical care should always be tailored to the individual patient. If you read something in this book that seems to conflict with your doctor's instructions, contact your doctor. Your doctor may have medically sound reasons for prescribing medication in a manner that may differ from the information presented in this book.

Also note that this book may not contain every drug or brand of drug currently prescribed in the treatment of child and adolescent psychiatric conditions.

If you have any questions about any medicine or treatment in this book, consult your doctor or pharmacist.

In addition, the patient names and cases used do not represent actual people, but are composite cases drawn from several sources.

DEDICATION

To our parents; our husbands, Soly and David; Ryan and Matthew; and Jennie, Fred, and Victor.

ACKNOWLEDGMENTS

The authors gratefully acknowledge the contribution of Edmund Blair Bolles to the text of this book.

Contents

INTRODUCTION   xi

PART I — THE DISRUPTIVE DISORDERS OF
         CHILDHOOD BEHAVIOR
    Chapter 1   *The Secret Handicap*   3
    Chapter 2   *Warning Signs*   14
    Chapter 3   *Psychiatric Evaluation*   21
    Chapter 4   *Treatment*   33

PART II — ATTENTION-DEFICIT HYPERACTIVITY
          DISORDER (ADHD)
    Chapter 5   *Living with ADHD*   55
    Chapter 6   *Educating Children with
                  ADHD*   67
    Chapter 7   *Treating ADHD*   75

PART III — CONDUCT DISORDER
    Chapter 8   *What Conduct Disorder Is*   89
    Chapter 9   *Treating Conduct Disorders* 107

PART IV — AFTER THEY ARE GROWN
    Chapter 10   *The Outcome*   117

SOURCES   125

INDEX   131

Introduction

As any adult knows, being a child has its ups and downs. But being a child whose temper, anger or behavior is out of control can be a consistently miserable experience. The child may be scolded, then punished and then ultimately ignored or shunted into a special school, correctional facility or institution. But now we know that the child whose behavior tortures others is often suffering inside, not fully understanding the source of his difficulties or why he is punished.

The number of children who suffer from what we call "disruptive disorders" may number in the millions. Yet only one in four may ever be properly diagnosed or even treated by a professional. In fact, there are over 50,000 children in mental health facilities. Almost one third of the patients in our hospital are under the age of 21.

In our years of practice we have seen a growing national crisis that was either ignored or swept under the carpet. Teenage suicide has risen 300% in the last three decades. At least 50% of all high school seniors have experimented with an illegal drug. Nine percent of all male children and two percent of young girls have Conduct Disorders (CD). Up to three percent of all school age children may suffer from an Attention-deficit Hyperactivity Disorder (ADHD).

Unfortunately parents with "difficult" children are sometimes unwilling to seek help for psychiatric disorders, yet the same parents don't hesitate to call a pediatrician for a "medical" problem. When confronted with the symptoms of behavior disorders, too many parents, and even professionals, may simply say, "He's o.k., he's just acting out," or "She's seeking attention. It's just a phase." But, psychiatric illness hurts just as much as a childhood disease.

Parents can be excused for their lack of knowledge. After all it's not easy to tell when acting out isn't acting, but instead can indicate signs of a problem like CD or ADHD. However, new diagnostic methods, new therapeutic guidelines, and new medications used properly have provided professionals with the tools they need to lessen a child's suffering.

We are starting to see some evidence that parents and professionals are recognizing the problem. A recent study indicated that 72% of parents of today's teenagers recognize that it's harder to be a teen today than when they grew up. More than half knew a child who was suffering from depression and more than 25% knew a teen who had tried to commit suicide.

Our society places considerable pressure on children to succeed today. A survey of high-achieving teens showed that 30% had considered suicide.

How to deal with these problems has also become controversial because many parents are afraid to have their children on a psychiatric medicine. Ritalin and Tofranil are being tried successfully on many children with disruptive disorders, yet these treatments are not complete answers. There are also many children who could benefit from psychophar-macological treatment and aren't being given that opportunity because their parents aren't seeking appropriate help. We've written this book to help parents and professional colleagues understand these childhood disorders. In this book we show:

- How to tell when "acting out" isn't acting and help your children receive proper, effective treatment when problems arise.
- How concomitant problems—substance abuse, depression, learning disabilities—impact on behavior of children and adolescents.
- How neurological evaluations, dietary modifications and psychopharmacology increase or decrease the chances of successful treatment.
- Whether children with ADHD or CD are more likely to develop major psychiatric disorders as adults.

We hope that by reading this book, both parents and mental health professionals will understand their role in reducing the suffering of children who are seemingly out of control, but in reality are crying out for proper help.

—Lynne W. Weisberg, M.D., Ph.D.
—Rosalie Greenberg, M.D.

PART I

The Disruptive Disorders of Childhood Behavior

CHAPTER 1

The Secret Handicap

"Mommy, my ear hurts..."

"I fell down and cut myself, Daddy..."

Most of the time children know when they hurt, and if they tell others about it they can usually count on a little sympathy and help. But sometimes children do not recognize their own difficulties. They are, for example, very slow to realize they are exhausted. A tired child is weepy and nearly impossible to control, but the child has no sense that something is wrong with himself. It is the world that has gone awry. Parents can recognize the problem and know the cure: Get the child to bed. The child protests, of course; the parents sigh and finally succeed. The next day normality has returned, although the child has no sense of having behaved impossibly the night before.

Some children suffer from this self-blindness most of the time. The world makes them restless, or it bores them, or it gets between them and their desires, or it forces them to attempt things they cannot do. It doesn't cross their minds that their restlessness and impulsivity might indicate that they have a problem. So they do not try to change themselves. It is the world they want to change. These children rebel by constantly trying to find things that interest them, and by not staying within the limits imposed on them.

Invariably, it is the people around such children who first notice a problem. A mother might see that her baby is having a hard time finding peace; a neighbor will notice that the toddler next door hollers constantly and smashes anything that comes within reach; a brother, sister, or playmate will know that a certain kid is no fun. When these children get older, teachers begin to complain that even the most rudimentary school discipline seems beyond them. Yet even as the number of alarmed or angry people grows, the children still may not recognize their own difficulties.

This view of oneself as an innocent victim can last long after ordinary children have developed a sense of their own responsibility. Two parents in an argument with their fourteen-year-old son became furious with the boy because he angrily threw a chair and smashed a window. The son was perplexed by their response. Why blame him, he wondered, when it was the parents who had made him so angry?

Indeed, parents do tend to accept some of this logic and will say to themselves that, ultimately, the child's behavior must be their fault. We hear parents say all the time, "If only I had been stricter," or, "If I were stronger, she would behave."

In our offices we often see the paradox of a relatively guilt-free child who creates mischief and guilt-ridden parents who have tried many things to correct the situation. We try to explain that the problem is not the parents' fault; their child has been born with a handicap.

Handicap? they ask. What handicap is that?

Their child is perfectly normal, they suddenly insist, forgetting that only minutes earlier they had described—usually in great distress—a child not like other children. When we point out this contradiction, the parents say that, yes, their child behaves "disruptively"—to use a nonjudgmental word—but does not have a handicap.

It *is* a startling word, but the child does have a handicap—one that, if left untreated, can lead to increasing difficulties. If this child had been born with an obvious physical handicap, the parents would respond more rationally. They would want to know if anything could be done, and upon hearing that treatment was available, they would say they wanted it. The idea of a behavioral handicap, however, is new, and many parents are still reluctant to accept the suggestion that a child who looks physically normal has an extra burden to bear.

When a child temporarily acts up, as when exhausted, parents can see the problem and respond without judging their child. They face the moment without saying to themselves that their child is hopeless, or has a bad attitude. They remember the real child behind the chaos of the moment. But a behavioral disorder is not temporary and does not pass after a good night's sleep. Its permanence makes it far harder to see the child behind the problem. Part of learning how to live with a behaviorally disordered child is learning to focus on the details of the child's behavior—by noting particular interests and talents, and by avoiding generalizations, especially negative generalizations, about motivation and attitude.

Getting beyond generalities to seeing a child who carries an extra burden requires a bit of adjustment in thinking. When parents come to our offices, they are worried about their child and unhappy with themselves. They see their child as willfully disobedient and see themselves as weak and ineffective. We tell them, no. Your child is no more deliberately irresponsible than a child with diabetes can be blamed for his condition—and the same lack of guilt holds true for the parents of the child.

Parents sometimes take this news a bit skeptically; old thought patterns do not die in an instant. They also wonder if we are speaking some trendy words that let everybody off the moral hook by forgetting about responsibility. But when they do finally accept that their child's behavior does not result from their failure, and when they understand that the purpose of treatment is to develop responsibility in the child instead of denying it in anybody, then the parents begin to see the diagnosis as good news. Their child is not hopelessly snared in a bad attitude. He has something wrong that can be treated, and he has the potential to grow up and lead a normal, happy, self-sustaining life of his own.

BEHAVIORAL DISORDERS AND SOCIETY

Anyone who has learned to live with a physical disorder can tell you that more than half the annoyance lies in the response of others to your situation. A person with a club foot may even forget about the difficulty, until he sees a pitying look on someone's face. "Handicapped," "limited," "not like the rest of us"—words like those may fill the stranger's mind.

Children with behavioral disorders are lucky in that regard. When their problem is under control, others do not even guess at the problem. The behaviorally handicapped carry no white cane that calls attention to themselves. But there is a price for this public invisibility. Before the disorder comes under control, people are not likely to believe that your child's disruptive behavior reflects a medical problem.

Away from the office we meet skeptics all the time. We even hear people say that the whole idea of a disruptive disorder is nonsense. The kids are just "rotten." After all, the symptoms of a behavioral disorder can turn up in every child. All children, especially preschoolers and infants, behave in disruptive ways. No one expects an infant to be disciplined or imagines that a toddler can obey all the rules. Furthermore, most children see themselves as innocents, and if their actions prove too disruptive, destructive, or aggressive, they blame others for the consequences. It is easy for people who do not have to live with these children to say the condition is normal and part of any child's behavior.

Unfortunately, they say these things to worried parents as well, and the parents tend to believe them. "Oh, they all do that," says a well-meaning neighbor. "My Billy used to do a lot worse, but he outgrew it." A concerned parent may welcome such remarks because they ease recurring fears.

When a disruptive child reaches an age where most children have outgrown such behavior, friends can still advise ignoring the problem. "Well, yes, he is a little immature for his age, but he'll outgrow it."

And when even the word "immature" no longer seems to cover the situation, neighbors and teachers may lose their sympathetic tone. "That child has a bad attitude," they begin to say. "He deliberately causes trouble. He likes to cause trouble." This final verdict reflects one of society's most deeply held assumptions. We act as we do because we choose to act that way. We are responsible for our actions.

Disruptive children, however, would be amazed to hear such an idea spelled out for them. One study found that children with disruptive disorders do not feel responsible for their actions and do not believe they control what they do. When children in elementary school hear a story about a child who behaves disruptively at school, all of the students can predict that the teacher will punish the unruly child, but there are two different explanations for the punishment. Most children will say that the teacher is worried that the behavior makes it hard for the others and that keeping order is part of a teacher's job. Children who are themselves disruptively disordered, however, offer a different explanation for the teacher's behavior. They say the teacher likes being the boss and dislikes the student.

Children can only develop a notion of responsibility if they believe that they are in control of their actions. If they view themselves as no more than boulders rolling down a cliff, they will not feel that any consequences are their fault, no matter how much havoc they wreak. Most children do not feel themselves to be loose boulders because they learn to get a grip on themselves. They insert judgments between an impulse and an action. And they come to assume that others can do likewise. So when someone acts as wildly as a runaway boulder, they figure that that person is spreading chaos on purpose.

The behavioral handicap of a disruptively disordered child is precisely an inability to put judgment between impulse and action. The reasons for this disorder are much discussed and disputed. It may be that problems with paying attention make it difficult for a child to develop judgment. Perhaps the child is so naturally restless that taking control of impulses is simply much more difficult for him. Or possibly there is some organic problem with those parts of the brain that control voluntary behavior. Despite this medical uncertainty, one important point is clear: Children with disruptive disorders cannot take control of their actions as easily as the rest of us can. They are capable of responsibility and need to be responsible, but the task can be difficult for them. Of course, having a handicap is not the same as being unable to function. A disruptive disorder is not a sentence of doom. It is an extra burden, an impediment to success, but a child can overcome it, especially with the increasingly sophisticated treatments that are now available.

DEVELOPING RESPONSIBILITY

The greatest difficulty arising from a disruptive disorder may be the challenge it presents to the development of social responsibility. In our experience, the most common age for the discovery of these disorders is at seven, when children enter the second grade. Disruptive classroom behavior at this age makes it increasingly evident that something is wrong. A seven-year-old who still cannot control his impulses is far behind his peers.

In traditional psychiatric terms, we say that seven-year-olds have usually developed a superego to balance their egos. In lay terms, we can say that the children have developed both a sense of themselves (an understanding of who they are and of what they want and need) along with a feeling of social responsibility. For example, seven-year-olds may always want to watch their favorite TV program (an example of their sense of themselves); however, they may also realize that they must occasionally give way to other family members' preferences (a sense of social responsibility). A disruptively disordered child usually has developed a sense of himself, but may not have developed fully a sense of responsibility. Some disruptively disordered children frequently know their desires and impulses to an unusually sharp degree, but without a fully developed sense of social responsibility, they may feel no obligation toward whatever impedes their wants. We must also add that there are other disruptively disordered children who *are* aware of their inability to function properly in society. But regardless of whether or not they are aware of their inability, these disruptively disordered children often do have a lack of social responsibility.

At this point a child's future is at terrible risk. One thing all children want is a sense of social inclusion. They want their parents' love and the friendship of their peers—without such support none of us could flourish. Soon after birth children begin responding positively to acts of love. Within a few months of birth they begin expressing their own pleasure at the recognition of others. An important social milestone typically appears in the third year, when children begin discovering many ways to interact with others their own age. The first signs of disruptive disorders sometimes become evident at this early age, sometimes even earlier. A child who does not learn how to act socially may try aggressively to force his playmates to act as he wishes. The playmates in turn begin to avoid the handicapped child, giving the child even less opportunity to develop social skills.

It is tragic to see five-year-olds who are desperate for friends and have no idea how to make them. Teachers may sometimes even complain that the child is *too social*, meaning that the child talks too much, follows others too much, and is too interested in peers when he should be quiet in class. But all this effort at finding friends does not necessarily make the child more popular. It can have just the opposite effect on children who want to listen to their teacher.

In the worst of circumstances, this situation is a prescription for catastrophe. As the disruptive children's sense of self continues to mature (they usually see themselves as misunderstood or inadequate, or blame others for their problems), their sense of responsibility remains embryonic. Their frustration over the continued rejection by peers and adults alike grows increasingly powerful. Occasionally children will, on their own, discover a way to get people to like them, but in most cases they become ever more remote from society. As their teen years approach, they can burst forth with violent and destructive behavior that brings them to the attention of the police. They can become "conduct disordered," a dangerous disruptive disorder in which their antisocial behavior interferes with even their daily life, and with the lives of others in a very negative way.

Conduct disorders are the last complication of

behavioral disorders that have taken many other bad turns; they are not a primary worry when we first see young children with disruptive disorders. But some failure to develop social skills and some lack of responsibility are commonplace. Often these failures are another source of guilt and anxiety for parents. Their child's continuing irresponsibility has made the parents angrier and more negative about the child. The parents feel guilty about their attitude, yet see no solution so long as their child remains irresponsible. Often, it is when parents feel themselves at the end of this rope that they first come to us and say, "I never thought I would visit a psychiatrist, especially one for my own child, but I just do not know what to do."

TAKING CONTROL

Treatment in these cases usually includes many steps. We must do something about the medical side of the problem, the behavioral disorder that is making the child so disruptive. We also have to develop a program to help the child learn the social skills that have gone undiscovered. Still another part of the treatment works to teach parents more effective ways of disciplining their child. Over a period of time, these steps can combine to turn an unhappy child with an uncertain future into a promising and smiling young person.

Before we even meet the child, however, we talk with the parents to hear their story. After listening to them report how they have come to their "wit's end," the first thing we normally stress is that their problem is *not* unusual. They may have never heard of such behavior in a child, but disruptive disorders are some of the most common psychiatric problems among schoolchildren. While exact statistics are not known, one of the most common conditions, Attention-deficit Hyperactivity Disorder, may affect three to five percent of the primary school age population.

Theoretically, given these statistics, it may mean that one child in twenty has a disruptive disorder. Or, almost every schoolroom is likely to have a child with a behavioral handicap! And unless you spent your first eight grades in a one-room schoolhouse with fifteen other children, it is almost certain that you attended a few classes with behaviorally handicapped classmates. In hindsight, most people can recall a few unusual incidents: the first-grader who was so unruly that he was expelled almost immediately; the new kid in the neighborhood all the other children quickly disliked because he fought too much; the tenth-grade clown who made everybody, even the teachers, laugh, but then always carried things too far. Once a person knows about disruptive disorders, he can say, "Oh, so that's what that was all about." It is not that those long-forgotten hyperactive classmates were bad or stupid (the popular explanations at the time); rather, they suffered from a common disorder that actually caused them to be out of control.

Recalling those old, briefly glimpsed cases of childhood difficulty has its tragic side as well. Until recently, nobody knew what to make of those children. What became of those affected? They were as much the victims of societal ignorance as they were of the behavioral disorder. Today we know that these cases are often quite treatable. During the past quarter century, we have acquired long experience in using different medications and forms of counseling. Some forms of therapy have been disappointing, but others have offered much help.

Treatment with medication, for example, has made great strides. Prescribing drugs for children may be controversial in some quarters, but some of the medicines normally used in cases of disruptive disorders constitute the safest, best studied, and most widely used class of drugs prescribed for children. Their role in treatment, and their safety, has been demonstrated in a number of studies. Counseling techniques for both family and child have also changed over time. While the old psychoanalytic forms of counseling were not especially helpful in cases of disruptive disorders, more recently developed techniques often appear more effective because they deal directly with the child's behavior and its impact on the child's environment. This type of therapy is more behaviorally oriented than the more traditional forms of psychotherapy.

None of us wants to learn that there is anything seriously wrong with our children. Each one of them is so important, so full of promise, that most parents resist the notion of trouble. But when the truth sets in, when we see that a child is behaviorally disordered, we have begun to overcome the secret handicap.

CHAPTER 2

Warning Signs

All children do things that alarm parents. They drift off into dreams; they act irresponsibly; they get "fidgety" on some solemn occasion; they throw tantrums which, if tried by an adult, would send people running for an ambulance. There is no single incident a person can point to and say, "There, that event proves your child is disordered." And really, no single behavior could prove the presence of a physical disorder either. A child does not have to be blind to miss seeing something on a table and does not have to be deaf to miss hearing his mother calling his name. Solitary incidents can bring a person to attention and raise questions, but by themselves they mean little. The important warning signs are patterns of behavior and an inability to function. Disruptive disorders can lead children to be disruptive in all kinds of situations where they would prefer to be well behaved.

If something has happened to make you wonder

14

bout your child's condition, it will take a medical valuation to make a final diagnosis. However, many eople hesitate to speak with a doctor about their hild's behavior. They wonder if they are making too uch of the normal rough and tumble of growing up. oints to consider before deciding to seek help inlude the child's:

- relationship with family members
- schoolwork
- peer relationships
- moods
- self-esteem
- aggressive outbursts
- athletic ability

These details are indicative because they are so outine. They get at the heart of the day-to-day happiness and satisfaction of your child's life. Many arents who begin to look for warning signs are eally looking for evidence that everything is okay, so ney search for things the child does successfully. Isually they can think of some notable examples and nen tell themselves, "My child cannot be hyperactive—he can sit for hours in front of the television." "He an enjoy computer video games and they require uch attention. There cannot be anything wrong." ut children with disruptive disorders often enjoy elevision and video games. Instead of searching for xamples of ordinary behavior, ask yourself how your hild functions in everyday situations.

Family relationships. The family relationships of he child with a disruptive disorder are often characerized by what behavioral psychologists call "coerion." These coercive, often adversarial relationships etween parent and child may include one or more of he following:

- verbal or physical abuse of or aggressiveness toward the child by either parent

- severe, often physical punishment as the main method of disciplining the child
- inconsistent discipline
- few supportive interactions among family members, with considerable marital tension and conflict and aggressiveness of one spouse toward the other
- attempts on the part of the child to injure sibling or parent
- poor supervision of the child
- child uses negative behavior (e.g., temper tantrums) to get his demands met and is successful with this method
- parent's failure to reward good behavior in positive manner, or to ignore good behavior
- possible associated parental drug and alcohol abuse and/or antisocial behavior

In our practice we often find that parents may inadvertently reinforce antisocial behavior either by their tendency to ignore good behavior or by their tendency to discipline the child in a harsh manner, thus providing a role model for aggressiveness. Power struggles and punishment are often the main element of discipline in the household of the child with a disruptive disorder. Parents are often unable to identify specific problem behaviors in their child which need changes and see the child in global terms as "bad."

Schoolwork. If a teacher reports that there is trouble at school, find out what is wrong. Disruptive behavior—often explained as immaturity, a little silliness, or excessive socializing—can interfere with learning. Careless, sloppy-looking schoolwork is another common result of acting without full control. Restlessness in only one school subject may reflect a dislike for that subject, but a general restlessness at school is another story.

Sudden changes in behavior are alarming. Two weeks of serious disruption can seem like an eternity ut no pediatric psychiatrist will diagnose a disruptive disorder unless symptoms have been visible for t least six months.

Peer relationships. An important tell-tale sign of a behavioral disorder is an inability to make friends. This problem is not a two-way street. Disruptively disordered children often have trouble keeping friends, but we cannot automatically rule out a disorder for any child with good friends. Even so, an important question a parent should consider when trying to judge their child's behavioral health is: Does the child have friends of his own age?

There are many reasons why a child, at any particular moment, might not have good friends. The child might have just arrived in a new neighborhood or school and does not yet know anyone; the child may spend time with an older brother or sister and play with their friends; the child is not yet three years old; the parents of playmates have some form of prejudice and have told their own children to stay away from a particular child; the child is so smart, he talks about things the other kids do not understand; the child is naturally shy and takes time to warm up to people, but eventually does break the ice.

Although these explanations can sometimes mask a problem, they usually explain the difficulty. Children need friends, and parents should help a lonely child find some, but these explanations suggest the problem is not a symptom of a disruptive disorder. There are some other explanations, however, that are more serious:

- Child is so eager to play he cannot wait his turn in games.
- Child plays too roughly with other kids.
- Child is a bully.
- Child takes things belonging to others.

- Child becomes restless during games and other kids complain he won't "play fair."

These are more serious signs of possible trouble. They are especially alarming if the problem crops up in more than one place. Sometimes a child gets off on a wrong foot with one group and can get back on track just by switching schools or playmates, but if the same difficulties appear at another school, the problem must be taken seriously. These items suggest that the child is trying to be a part of the social scene, but does not know how. This situation does not always mean that the child has a disruptive disorder, but it is always serious and should be resolved. Older children will sometimes reject the friendship of a disruptively disordered child within hours of their first meeting.

Moods. Sudden mood swings are another warning sign of potential trouble. Children with this characteristic are commonly labeled with a host of unflattering terms. One especially popular one is "spoiled," a word that automatically puts parents on the defensive because it blames the parents for the child's problem behavior. We often hear the word used to describe:

- Children who get overexcited and loud, and are hard to calm down.
- Irritable children who suddenly turn a happy moment into a grouchy one.
- Children who have "yelling and screaming fits," tantrums so unrestrained they would embarrass another child half their age.
- Children who suddenly become stubborn and refuse to cooperate with some new plan of action.

Besides "spoiled," these children may be called "brats" and "immature." Patterns of such behavior are an important warning sign of possible trouble.

Self-esteem. Children should like themselves and

think well of themselves. If they do not, something is wrong. Do not simply dismiss low self-esteem as "sensitivity" or "a phase." Once it is badly shaken, recovering one's self-esteem can take years. Dislike of self is an important warning sign that a child is treated negatively too often. Disruptively disordered children may not feel that there is anything wrong in their behavior, but because so many people—peers, teachers, neighbors, and parents—react against them, these children eventually do conclude that there must be something wrong with themselves.

Aggressive outbursts. Fights, especially among boys, may occasionally occur. Some children, however, have more than their share of fights. These scrappers may explain themselves by saying the other guy always starts it, and the justification may be true, up to a point. Physically awkward, socially unskilled children are favorite targets for teasing by their peers. Parents tend naturally to stick up for their offspring and to believe that their own child is more sinned against than sinning. But a child who regularly gets into fights, even if only because he regularly "fights back," raises a question mark. About the only mitigating circumstance is a strong dislike between two particular children. When most of the fighting is between your child and one other—a brother, sister, or a particularly aggravating classmate—the problem may be less ominous. Of course, recurring fights must be dealt with, but they are usually one more detail in growing up. When considering disruptive disorders, a generalized aggression is more of a warning of trouble than a focused anger.

One especially alarming type of aggression is anything hurtful that seems sadistic or planned. Childhood fights are usually spontaneous eruptions of emotion. Desire, anger, or impatience overwhelms the moment. Actions that do harm without originating as a response to some other impulse are serious warning signs that a child may be developing antisocial skills. The situation should be looked at.

Athletic ability. Some children are better at playing games than others. Preschoolers are generally more enthusiastic than skilled, and falling down is the common fate of young runners. Scabby knees are part of being young. Yet some children are more clumsy than others. They fall down more often and simply lack grace. When they enter school they do not progress in sports as well as their classmates, and by fifth or sixth grade they are commonly picked last when it comes to choosing up sides for a team. Inexperience and a lack of skill may explain the problem. It can also be that a child, even a bright child, is not imaginative when it comes to sports and plays more like a robot than a star. Disruptively disordered children, however, are often clumsy because their feet get ahead of their purposes or they may have mild coordination problems. To use a phrase popular with sports broadcasters, they can "lack concentration." They may be all action and give no thought to what they are doing. In such cases a person throws but throws wildly, kicks energetically but not well, catches and then drops a ball. Even the greatest athletes sometimes have these lapses, but in disruptively disordered children they are not that uncommon.

CHAPTER 3

Psychiatric Evaluation

Parents come to us for many reasons. "The teacher says he is hyperactive," parents sometimes report. Other times a parent will say, "The teacher says he is not hyperactive, but something is wrong." We also hear what neighbors and relatives have said, and what parents have read in books or seen on television. Obviously, most parents who visit us are worried, and they have many questions for which they want prompt answers. But before we can satisfactorily answer their questions, it takes a careful examination of many factors to make a diagnosis.

During the past twenty years, psychiatry has developed more precise criteria for evaluating a child's condition and for distinguishing between individual disruptive disorders. That growing precision is the major reason for the changing names given various conditions. For example, in the past, psychiatrists would talk about "minimal brain damage"—but no specific area of brain damage could be found. Other names, such as "minimal brain dysfunction" and, later, "the hyperactive child," were used. The latter name focused more directly on the nonspecific symptom of hyperactivity. Today, child psychiatrists have broadened this classification to be the *Attention-deficit Hyperactivity Disorder (ADHD)* described in the *Diagnostic and Statistical Manual of Mental Disorders,* Third Edition, Revised (or DSM-III-R for short). This new classification does not attempt to describe the cause of the condition, but rather describes symptoms in a nonjudgmental fashion. Two other disruptive disorders included in DSM-III-R are called *Conduct Disorder* and *Oppositional Defiant Disorder.* A psychiatric evaluation of a disruptive child tries to find an explanation for the behavior. Only sometimes do we find that the problem is simply a disruptive disorder. In our experience, the initial evaluation typically requires about three hours of consultation, and is usually done over a few visits. First we meet with a parent or parents alone. Next we interview the child alone. Then we meet with both parent and child together.

We also like to hear from a child's teacher. The most frequent means of contact is through a questionnaire and telephone discussion. Rarely will a parent object to getting the school involved in the evaluation, but it does occur sometimes. We respect parents' wishes, but it can make determining the diagnosis that much more difficult and uncertain. Such a parent is usually worried that the teacher and school will be prejudiced against the child if word of the psychiatric consultation spreads. In our experience, however, just the opposite occurs. Schools that know a disruptive child is receiving professional help tend to look favorably on the child and his prospects. Of course we never divulge to a teacher or school principal anything learned in confidence about the child. We are only hoping to gain as full a picture of the child's life and history as possible. If we feel that there is something that would be very important for the school to know, we always discuss this with the parents and obtain their consent before informing the school.

CHECKING YOUR CHILD'S HISTORY

Presentation. A psychiatric evaluation begins the same way any other medical examination starts, with a discussion of what has led to seeking medical help. We want to hear the parents' description of the behaviors that trouble them and learn the history of each one of these behaviors. How long have they been going on? Have they recently gotten worse? Was it a last straw that led the parents to our offices or was there a sudden crisis?

Each behavior raises questions as a doctor probes for details that will help distinguish between similar-sounding symptoms. We also try to get a sense of the child behind the words. When different families describe how their child disrupts home and school, they often choose similar words and phrases, even though each child is unique. During this first part of the consultation, we try to get a clear picture of the individual child.

Birth and developmental history. Once the parents have outlined the concerns that brought them to the office, we like to obtain a full account of the child's development. These details can help rule out other possible explanations for the difficulty, and they can point our thinking in particular directions.

Disruptive disorders often begin early, although it usually takes hindsight to recognize the earliest signs. When they first appear they are ambiguous. Parents will recall that teachers used to say the child was "too social" (talked too much in class) or "immature" (not socially in control) or "a little silly" (behaved inappropriately). Plenty of children are weak at self-control at first. It is only by looking backward that a parent will see that the child did not outgrow the tendency.

Also, we like to know what we call "developmen-

tal milestones." When did the child walk? When did
he begin to talk? Was he a good eater? Was she a
good sleeper? What kind of baby was he—playful,
active, passive, fussy, et cetera? Did the parents ever
raise questions with their pediatrician about the
child's behavior? Did symptoms appear suddenly? If
yes, why? Parents sometimes explain a change as just
a phase. "It's just adolescence," we sometimes hear,
or, "He is having to adjust to a new _____ (pick one:
school, teacher, home)." But phases and adjustments
do not persist. We take symptoms that last six months
or more seriously. It always seems sad when a child
has been having trouble in school for years and a
parent says, "I thought it was just part of being a
teenager."

Medical history. Has the youngster ever had any
serious illness? Has the child ever been hospitalized?
If yes, when, why, and for how long? Is there any
history of allergies (a crucial question if medication
is necessary)? Has the child ever suffered a head
injury, loss of consciousness, or seizures? Answers to
these questions may provide us with valuable information that may reveal the conditions that contributed to or caused the child's present problem.

School history. It is important to go over school
history year by year, starting with whenever the child
began school, be it nursery school, kindergarten, or
first grade. How has the child responded to the
increasing structure of the classroom? How is the
child doing academically? What does the teacher say
about him? How are the child's social relationships
in school? Do his peers see him as too immature, too
unwilling to wait his turn, or too aggressive? Occasionally, however, disruptive children are admired by
their peers, who see the disrupter as doing things
they do not have the nerve to do themselves. Often, of
course, parents come to us because they are concerned that their child is doing worse and worse in
school, lagging further behind with no apparent hope
of ever catching up. If schoolwork is a serious prob-

lem, we want to be sure the child does not have a learning disability. A child with dyslexia, for example, may find trying to read so frustrating that he quits paying attention to lessons. However, for a dyslexic child, the poor attention span in class will not be accompanied by other symptoms of a disruptive disorder, unless the child suffers from both disorders.

Home history. What are the family relationships like? Who is the child close to, or distant from? What are the methods of disciplining bad behavior? How has difficult behavior been dealt with before? Did anything work? Even a little? How does the child's home behavior compare with school behavior? Is it better or worse? Has the household become enmeshed in a negative cycle? Families often slip into systems in which the parents become increasingly irritated by their child's disruptive behavior, and the child's self-esteem declines almost from week to week.

Family history. An examination should discover as much as possible about the family's medical and psychiatric history. Have there been major illnesses in the family? Has anyone had a psychiatric disorder? A learning disability? A history of hyperactivity? Trouble with the law, or school problems? Parents often see this part of the consultation as particularly sensitive, for it probes areas that may never have been revealed to the child. A mother may say, "Well, my brother committed suicide, but I do not want my children to know that their uncle died that way." One reason we meet first with the parents alone and exclude the child is so that parents can speak freely. We need to know as much as possible, both to make a diagnosis and to prescribe treatment.

CHECKING YOUR CHILD

The initial interview with the child begins with an assessment of the child's appearance. Is he small or tall for his age? Is he neatly or sloppily dressed? How someone dresses—even a child—indicates how that person approaches the world. We also observe if the child needs to have his parents with him. Can the child talk freely alone? Does he appear angry, depressed, or agitated? With these observations made, we will then proceed with the interview.

Discussions with the child depend to some extent on his age. We want to know how children feel about themselves, their family, school, peers and what they think their problem is. This last question can be especially revealing, because children often have a remarkably different view from their parents. The parents see the child as disruptive, but the child may see the problem as parents who are unreasonably touchy about every little thing. The parents see the child as deliberately causing trouble; the child complains that it is unfair to blame him for things he does not do, or if he does them, it's not his fault. Part of the conference with the child may be devoted to reassuring him that the problem is not that he is bad, but that he needs help in learning how to control what he does so people will not get so mad at him.

We usually check the child for signs of mood disorder, such as depression or mania. We inquire about his sleep, appetite, concentration, and ability to have fun. We ask about suicidal or homicidal thoughts or behavior. Questions we may ask ourselves include:

- Does the child confuse fantasy and reality?
- Does the child see or hear things that are not present?
- How good is the child's memory?
- Does the child have an adequate fund of knowledge?

The first two questions reflect the fact that hyperactive children often have hyperactive imaginations. They may construct incredibly creative tales and act as if they are real—while knowing that they are fantasy. However, other children may actually be suffering from hallucinations (seeing or hearing imaginary things) or delusions (believing in false ideas).

The last two questions may indicate a learning problem in school—obviously if a child has trouble with memory, then learning ability will be limited. Similarly, a learning problem may exist if the child's overall knowledge level is weak.

In addition, basic math, cognitive, and judgment skills are assessed. Throughout the interview, the psychiatrist explores the child's inner feelings and experiences that the parent may be unaware of. Clearly the psychiatric evaluation covers a wide range of areas, areas that may help the psychiatrist diagnose and, if necessary, treat the child's problem.

Physical exam. The evaluation of a child includes a physical assessment, beginning with a record of the child's blood pressure, pulse, height, and weight. This information is especially important if medication is later used in treatment, since medication may have an effect on these readings. We also conduct a brief neurological survey designed to uncover what we call "soft signs." These soft signs do not indicate a specific neurological problem, but they may indicate an abnormality in the child's nervous system that may be associated with ADHD, or other mental disorders. An example of a soft sign might be if the child confuses right and left sides.

Frequently, a wide range of laboratory tests may be ordered, including blood, liver, kidney, and thyroid tests. These tests usually provide valuable information that can be applied to the diagnosis or treatment of the child's condition. For example, a youngster who appears to be overly active, agitated, or depressed may be suffering from a thyroid abnormality, a type of problem that responds well to medical treatment.

Occasionally, an electroencephalogram (EEG) may be necessary if the situation suggests that the child may be suffering from a seizure disorder. Similarly, depending upon the child's initial evaluation, an electrocardiogram (ECG) may be necessary before prescribing any medication that can affect the heart.

Assessment scales. There are also several standardized scales for assessing behavior in different settings. Two of the most popular measures are the Conners Abbreviated Parent Rating Scale and the Conners Teacher Rating Scale. These scales rate the child's behavior as observed by the parents at home and teacher at school. They help compare children much as a line of statistics guides a sports fan. The whole story is not in that line, but it gives a general sense of the situation.

THE DIAGNOSIS

After considering all the information gathered, the examiner then offers psychiatric judgment about the nature of the problem. The diagnosis may point to something physical—e.g., a seizure disorder—or the examiner may say there is nothing wrong with the child. Behavior that seems exasperating can still be within the normal range for children at a particular age, especially when viewed within the context of the child's full history. Disruptive behavior may also reflect a disorganized home in which the child receives no clear guidance on how to behave responsibly. Here the whole family may benefit from treatment. Or the diagnosis may confirm a disruptive disorder. How does an examiner turn those discussions and tests into such a conclusion?

Attention-deficit Hyperactivity Disorder (ADHD) is diagnosed when the psychiatrist observes the presence of certain behaviors, as listed in DSM-III-R. These behaviors are:

ADHD CRITERIA

Note: Consider a criterion met only if the behavior is considerably more frequent than that of most people of the same mental age.

A. A disturbance of at least six months during which at least eight of the following are present:

   (1) often fidgets with hands or feet or squirms in seat (in adolescents, may be limited to subjective feelings of restlessness)
   (2) has difficulty remaining seated when required to do so
   (3) is easily distracted by extraneous stimuli
   (4) has difficulty awaiting turn in games or group situations
   (5) often blurts out answers to questions before they have been completed
   (6) has difficulty following through on instructions from others (not due to oppositional behavior or failure of comprehension), e.g., fails to finish chores
   (7) has difficulty sustaining attention in tasks or play activities
   (8) often shifts from one uncompleted activity to another
   (9) has difficulty playing quietly
   (10) often talks excessively
   (11) often interrupts or intrudes on others, e.g., butts into other children's games
   (12) often does not seem to listen to what is being said to him or her
   (13) often loses things necessary for tasks or activities at school or at home (e.g., toys, pencils, books, assignments)
   (14) often engages in physically dangerous activities without considering possible consequences (not for the purpose of thrill-seeking), e.g., runs into street without looking

B. Onset before the age of seven.

C. Does not meet the criteria for a Pervasive Developmental Disorder (PDD). The DSM-III-R describes PDD as a disorder involving basic psychological functions that affects the development of social skills and language. The most common form of PDD is Infantile Autism.

At least eight of these symptoms must be present, and must have occurred before the age of seven. One must remember that making the correct diagnosis is more than just treating the above symptoms as a checklist. A psychiatrist should always use good clinical judgment and must eliminate other conditions (such as a thyroid disease) that may mimic a psychiatric disorder. Other children may appear to be overactive, but are really displaying a very active but natural level of activity appropriate for their age. Also, other psychiatric conditions, such as an agitated depression, may appear erroneously to be ADHD.

Oppositional Defiant Disorder (ODD) refers to the youngster who exhibits negative, hostile, and defiant behavior, without seriously violating the rights of others. To make the diagnosis of ODD, according to DSM-III-R, the youngster must meet the criteria described below.

ODD CRITERIA

Note: Consider a criterion met only if the behavior is considerably more frequent than that of most people of the same mental age.

A. A disturbance of at least six months during which at least five of the following are present:

   (1) often loses temper
   (2) often argues with adults
   (3) often actively defies or refuses adult requests or rules, e.g., refuses to do chores at home

(4) often deliberately does things that annoy other people, e.g., grabs other children's hats
(5) often blames others for his or her own mistakes
(6) is often touchy or easily annoyed by others
(7) is often angry and resentful
(8) is often spiteful or vindictive
(9) often swears or uses obscene language

B. Does not meet the criteria for Conduct Disorder, and does not occur exclusively during the course of a psychotic disorder, Dysthymia, or a Major Depressive, Hypomanic, or Manic Episode.

As with the diagnosis of ADHD, other psychiatric and physical diagnoses should be ruled out before making a diagnosis of ODD.

Conduct Disorder (CD) is a more serious disruptive disorder. CD refers to a behavior pattern in which the youngster violates the rights of others as well as the societal norms appropriate for his age. A child with CD may repeatedly engage in vandalism, theft, and fighting. The diagnostic criteria for CD include:

CD CRITERIA

A. A disturbance of conduct lasting at least six months, during which at least three of the following have been present:

(1) has stolen without confrontation of a victim on more than one occasion (including forgery)
(2) has run away from home overnight at least twice while living in parental or parental surrogate home (or once without returning)
(3) often lies (other than to avoid physical or sexual abuse)
(4) has deliberately engaged in fire-setting
(5) is often truant from school (for older person, absent from work)

(6) has broken into someone else's house, building, or car
(7) has deliberately destroyed others' property (other than by fire-setting)
(8) has been physically cruel to animals
(9) has forced someone into sexual activity with him or her
(10) has used a weapon in more than one fight
(11) often initiates physical fights
(12) has stolen with confrontation of a victim (e.g., mugging, purse-snatching, extortion, armed robbery)
(13) has been physically cruel to people

B. If 18 or older, does not meet criteria for Antisocial Personality Disorder.

We must stress that in making the proper diagnosis for any of these disruptive disorders, other psychiatric and physical disorders must be eliminated. A proper diagnosis is the most important step toward creating a good treatment plan.

CHAPTER 4

Treatment

In general, medical conditions are more often controlled than cured. Control means learning to live with a disorder and working to prevent it from becoming even more damaging.

The treatment of disruptive disorders usually has this purpose. At the time of diagnosis, no one can know whether the disorder will endure for months or for years, but the doctor, family, and patient can strive to get a grip on its progress. That is the goal of treating a disruptive disorder: taking charge of the situation so that you and your child control the disorder—and the disorder no longer controls you.

Sometimes parents ask what good medicine is if it cannot cure a problem. The answer comes by looking at cases that continue untreated:

Sally's problems only became alarming when she was twelve.

True, she had not done well in school and

was sometimes defiantly disobedient at home, but her parents just assumed that was her way. In the seventh grade, however, she shocked her parents by becoming promiscuous with high-school boys. After more than a year of trouble her parents took her for a psychiatric examination. A pediatric psychiatrist diagnosed a disruptive disorder with complicating factors arising from the long delay in seeking treatment.

Ron's third-grade teacher was so alarmed by his behavior that she insisted he see a doctor before being allowed to return to school. Ron's father, however, objected, saying that he had been the same way when he was that age and had outgrown it.

Instead of seeing a doctor, Ron was placed in a new school. Over time his condition only worsened. His school marks were consistently low. He began getting into deeper trouble, having his first scrape with the law when he was eleven. By the time he was fifteen and ordered by a court to receive a psychiatric evaluation, several police officers were already familiar with Ron's history.

In each of these examples the disorder controls the destiny of the children and their families. The outcome is left up to the mercy of the disorder itself.

Compare those cases with Arthur's: He was diagnosed as having a disruptive disorder when he was still in first grade, and eleven years later, at age seventeen, he is still undergoing treatment. He has not been cured. Even on a teen tour, where people know little of his history, his chaperones can see something is wrong if Arthur skips his medication for a few days. The disorder, however, is under control. He is a happy young man, with good school marks, many friends, a zest for life, and he suffers from none of the antisocial complications that can make a disruptive disorder increasingly worrisome. Arthur's father sometimes looks back on the years of treatment with still no end in sight and complains about the money and energy expended; we reply simply that it was worth it all. Arthur is a beautiful boy, blossoming into young manhood with good friends and without a conduct disorder. For some lucky people that life seems to come naturally. For Arthur it has taken treatment, but he has gotten there.

WHAT TREATMENT IS

A treatment is a plan to take control of the disorder. If a full evaluation ends in the diagnosis of a disruptive disorder, the family and doctor should work together to develop a treatment suited to their situation. Children are always individuals, and any plan will begin with a search to discover what works in your child's case. Experience has shown us a variety of approaches, but it may take a little time to discover which one works best for your child. That uncertainty makes it important to stick with a plan until you learn how it works. It can be frustrating to try something and see no progress, but slowly you and the doctor are learning how to control the disorder. Breaking with a plan before its outcome is clear simply surrenders control back to the disorder.

Because the future of the disorder is uncertain, the plan must be flexible enough to allow for various possibilities.

If a child will naturally outgrow the problem, the treatment must allow that growth. At the same time, treatment should prevent the disorder from doing further damage to the child, family, and society.

If the disorder proves persistent, the treatment must be able to control its progress over a long time. In these cases, treatment must both prevent the development of complicating damage to the child's personality and behavior and help the family come to terms with the persistence of a psychiatric disorder.

Treatment resembles a military campaign in which the general does not know if he is in for a lightning conquest or for a long siege. Flexibility is the key. Hope for the quick result, but always be ready for the longer effort. And if you settle down for a long term, never forget that quick actions may again be necessary.

FAMILY TREATMENT

Some older treatments of disruptive disorders rested on the assumption that problems within the family were the cause of the disorder. We do not believe that families are the root cause of disruptive disorders, but difficulties within a family—some of which spring from living with a disruptive child—can complicate the situation. Families often arrive in our offices in a state of chaos and confusion. Their child's behavior has taken such control of their household that no one knows what to think or do. Their child is out of control, their marriage is strained, and the other children are disrupted as well. Keeping the family strong is important in treating the disorder.

Parents, especially mothers, tend to believe they should be able to raise their children on their own. This Ozzie-and-Harriet form of parenting has been rare historically, but modern America considers it normal. The single-handed approach to parenting is especially trying when children present unusual difficulties. With disruptive children, it has been said that a "normal amount of mothering is not enough." "A normal amount of mothering" is plenty of mothering, and when that is not enough, parents are quickly overwhelmed. Studies show that a family's ability to cope with a disruptive child increases as the mother's support system outside the home increases. Friends, kinfolk, and doctors can be part of that system, and parents should learn to use it. Treatment for families begins with first, the family realizing that they are not totally responsible for the disruptive child's problems and second, learning to accept treatment. Until these steps are taken, many of the specific problems that need attention will persist and even harden.

Typical family problems include:

Impulse to harm child. Sometimes parents first come to us because they are so frustrated they fear they will seriously abuse their disruptive child. Treatment should include ways of controlling this temptation. One prudent policy is a straight "no spanking" rule, because the temptation to keep on hitting can become too strong.

Blaming one another. It is rare for two parents to agree completely on how to raise children, but when a child fares well enough, most people are able to take a live-and-let-live attitude toward the other parent's practices. When something goes wrong, however, it is more difficult to look so tolerantly on the other parent's child-rearing idiosyncrasies. Treatment should develop an approach that both parents can agree on. Perfect agreement is still unlikely, but the pair can work within a common frame.

Unreasonable expectations. Much of the frustration of raising a disruptive child comes from expecting behavior that in this case is simply impossible. Treatment should include help with forming realistic standards, so parents are not endlessly frustrated and children are not pushed to meet expectations they cannot attain. Parents should learn to recognize when their expectations soar too high. Frequent frustration and disappointment means parents should take a step back to ask if they are pushing for too much.

Obsession. It is easy to let a disruptive child dominate all family life. Even when parents take a break, go to a movie, and relax in a restaurant afterwards, they may still talk and think about what they can do for their disruptive child. Treatment should help them learn ways to enjoy themselves without always worrying about their child. Such an approach is not selfish. Children do not benefit from being raised by frustrated parents who think of nothing but their children's problems.

Sibling discontent. Families sometimes first come to us because a state of guerrilla warfare exists between the children. Treatment should help siblings learn how to get along with their disruptive brother or sister, how to encourage proper behavior, and how to handle those embarrassing moments when a friend asks, "How come your brother is so weird?"

Families at risk. Although the future of each case of disruptive disorder is unpredictable, some children are at greater risk for worsening behavior. Strained marriages, alcoholism, chronic unemployment, and economic hardship are stresses that affect even healthy children. Treatment for families with these problems should try to include help in these areas.

Despair. Families may feel they have done all they can. Treatment should encourage the parents as well as the child to realize that, in time, they will be able to do more than currently seems possible. Do not aim for the sky. Do the little you know you can do, and having seen yourself do that, do a little more.

Emotion. When they arrive for treatment parents often are both angry with their child for being so disruptive and frightened for his future. These emotions may be eased temporarily by a few wise words and buck-up encouragement, but the enduring solution comes through successful treatment. As treatment begins to make some headway and parents feel themselves getting some control of the situation, the anger and fear that comes from being without control recedes.

Family treatment cannot help with everything. There are still going to be times when you are embarrassed by your child's public behavior. There are still going to be those arrogant relatives who brag about their child's perfect manners and use your child's disorder as a club to put you down.

here are still going to be people next door who once
read a book on psychology and have fourteen fancy
ways of saying that it's all the parents' fault. But a
treatment plan that includes a good family intervention program has an interesting side effect. These
aggravations do not go away, and they do not cease to
be irritating, but they no longer cause panic and
despair. As the family feels itself taking greater control, the slings and arrows of outrageous neighbors
matter less and less.

SCHOOL TREATMENT

Usually a plan will include some role for the school.
In most (but not all) cases, disruptive children have a
harder time with school routine than with home life.
Sometimes treatment will include placing a child in
a special school. More often, disruptive children continue within their established school system, but
they may need more help. Treating your child at
school requires some special school-family cooperation. If school cooperation turns out to be impossible, you may consider looking for a better school.

Establishing contact. Once a treatment plan is
developed, parents should discuss the plan with the
school. You can meet with your child's teacher to
discuss the disorder and the treatment. It may also
help to have the teacher meet with you and the
school psychologist. Explain the situation clearly, but
do not dwell on the negatives. Let the teacher understand the progress that has been made.

Explain directly that the problem is not necessarily one of "poor motivation" or "lack of caring,"
and urge the teacher to think about helping a handicapped child. The school's cooperation with any medication aspect of the treatment plan is important, and
parents should insist upon getting cooperation.

If the teacher is cooperative, your child can be in
for an especially fine school year. Teachers who can

see beyond the disorder to the child can be major influences in helping your child develop a sense of self-worth and self-control as well as helping the child find new interests.

Providing structure. We hear parents say sometimes, "I should send him to military school. They'll teach discipline." The thought makes us cringe. A school where standards and expectations of discipline are unusually high is just the place to guarantee another failing experience for your child. The idea of giving more structure to the child is good, but the structure should be based on more realistic expectations. The more cut-and-dried the school routine, and the more precise the instructions, the better.

You should introduce strong structure in homework, too. Have a fixed routine, time, and place for doing homework. Get a big wall calendar for marking due dates for any special projects or field trips. Use different folders for completed assignments and ongoing work. The routine should also include scheduled breaks. Make special efforts to get your child to write down homework assignments as they are given. (If possible, the teacher should keep a special eye out for this part of classwork.) Ask the teacher to help develop an end-of-the-school-day routine in which your child selects the books needed for that day's homework.

If your child repeatedly forgets to bring home the necessary books, see if the school will let you have a second set for home. A second set may seem like an extraordinary idea, but it exchanges the frustrated sense of being out of control for the more satisfying feeling of being in charge and seeing that homework gets done.

Special programs. Some schools have special programs for helping disruptive children. The simplest program has teachers praise children for appropriate behavior. It helps disruptive students immeasurably when their good conduct is promptly and loudly encouraged.

• A more elaborate program of rewards gives children points for good behavior and takes them away or does not allow them to earn extra points for poor behavior. These points should be something the children can touch and see, like play money. When they gain enough points, they can trade them in for some other reward. This system works well and has been adopted by some schools. Some schools have adopted a program known as the Primary Mental Health Project (PMHP) to work with children who are at risk for developing serious antisocial disorders. This school project concentrates on developing a strong accepting relationship with the individual child. Followup studies of the program indicate that its benefits are long-lasting; a more detailed description of this program is provided on page 99.

INDIVIDUAL TREATMENT

Many treatment plans include individual counseling and therapy for the disruptive child. Treatment usually focuses on issues of self-control and self-esteem. At one time individual therapy was the primary part of a treatment plan, but results at times have been disappointing. We agree with the modern consensus that disruptive disorders derive from a biological problem in the brain—a problem that cannot be treated exclusively by talking and feeling. Individual treatment may, however, help overcome some secondary effects of the disorder, and definitely has a role in the treatment of many youngsters.

MEDICATION AND MODIFICATION: TWO COMMON TREATMENTS

Medication

The most dramatic control in our clinical experience has come through medication. During recent decades psychiatry has undergone a quiet revolution, as it has switched from simply treating emotional or psychological problems to treating the complete body. We believe that many disruptive disorders arise because of some inborn physiological problems. We have seen the disorders respond to medicine more quickly and decisively than to any other form of treatment. In many cases medication is the mainstay of a treatment plan, with the other parts of the plan supporting the medication program.

Unfortunately, some individuals respond negatively to the advent of medication in psychiatry. In the next section, let us consider some common objections to the use of medication.

Is medication an insult? Nobody wants to hear that their child's mental abilities are disordered, but as we learn more about the brain and about learning, we are discovering that each brain is unique. Brains turn out to be like fingerprints: patterns recur, but the details for each person are always different. Each difference gives us our own set of abilities and disabilities. We make of these gifts what we can, but being insulted by the suggestion that we are born with strengths and weaknesses seems foolish.

Is medication a distraction? Parents of patients often say to us, "I would rather treat the real problem." By "real problem" they usually mean the unconscious emotional or moral failing (either theirs or their child's) that they believe is really behind their child's disorder. The problem endured by disruptive children is that they have difficulty controlling their impulses. Medication often helps them get that control. Most of us have seen this approach work in one common type of case that we are all familiar with: the headache sufferer. People with headaches may become ill-tempered and shout at their colleagues. Most often, their behavior improves simply by taking an aspirin, or other pain reliever, that stops the headache. The medication was not a distraction; it simply helped manage and relieve the discomfort.

Does medication interfere where we should not interfere? Sometimes parents acknowledge that even though they understand their child has difficulty and that their problem is not a moral one, the idea of taking pills for a behavioral problem is upsetting. For some people, the use of psychiatric medication violates the natural spirituality of the mind.

We must confess to a sense of exasperation when we hear this argument. Medication for disruptive disorders, when properly administered, helps children realize their full potential in life, including their spiritual natures. Many people believe that spirituality is expressed through our bodies, as in the act of bringing hands together in prayer. That physical action has spiritual meaning. Suppose, however, a person is so crippled with arthritis that clasping the hands is no longer possible. Medication that ends the pain and permits the action helps, not hinders, spiritual expression. Spirituality begins with taking responsibility for one's own actions. How can a medication that helps a child take more responsibility interfere with his spiritual nature?

Understanding Medication

Prescription. A variety of medicines may be prescribed. If your doctor prescribes a medication, the choice will depend on the exact diagnosis and your child's medical history. We shall discuss some of these drugs in individual detail in later chapters. Many of the medications prescribed for disruptive disorders are stimulants, or actually psychostimulants. This prescription sometimes surprises parents, who feel that their child is active enough already. In children, however, stimulants can help the youngster sit still better and help improve the child's concentration.

Initiation. Usually the starting dosage of a medication will be minimal, so the doctor can better regulate the effects. The dosage may be increased, if necessary, until it reaches a level at which full benefits can be expected. Sometimes a medication does not work for a particular child, or its side effects are too strong. In these cases, the doctor may try an alternate medication. A satisfactory medication is usually found, although not always on the first try. This process can be frustrating because it may take a month or longer to conclude that the results are unsatisfactory. Medical treatment for disruptive disorders, however, is more often a marathon than a sprint, and slow starts do not mean bad finishes.

Maintenance. Once a suitable drug and dosage has been identified, taking the medication becomes a matter of routine. You should have fixed times for your child to take the medicine. One popular time is right after meals. Sometimes a medicine reduces a child's appetite, so it will be important to work out the timing of the medication in relation to mealtimes.

Combined medication. Medications may produce a variety of effects, some welcome, others less so. To balance these effects, a doctor will sometimes prescribe other medications.

Tolerance. Parents may notice that a particular medication no longer works as effectively as before. Sometimes the change can be handled by increasing the dosage. Other times the solution is to switch to a different medication.

Drug rebound. At the end of the day, as the stimulant medication wears off, some children become even more irritable and active than usual. Sometimes, small doses of the medication can be taken just after returning home from school to decrease the rebound effect.

Drug vacations. Depending on the nature of the disorder, some children can halt their use of stimulant medication during the summer break from school. In general, the medication should be withdrawn gradually, since with some medications, abruptly stopping the medication can produce uncomfortable effects.

Resuming maintenance. Although a drug vacation may show that a child no longer needs this medication, many other children must resume the treatment. These times can be disappointing for child and parent alike, as they remind everyone that the treatment merely controls the symptoms, but does not cure them. It can be hard to see the problems prevented and the difficulties that have been avoided, until you remind yourself that your child is returning to medication because it really does make things better.

General Principles of Medication

Parents and medication. The *Clinical Guide to Child Psychiatry* states bluntly, "The parents form the key to success in the treatment of the child with psychoactive drugs." It is up to them to see that their child takes the medication at the right time, and to see that the school cooperates in the treatment. Sometimes parents will bring a sixteen-year-old into our offices and boast that they have proudly kept their child off pills that were recommended to them nine or ten years earlier. The parents do not even seem to notice they are talking of having allowed the disorder to continue out of control for a decade. In the end, it is the parents' responsibility to maintain the treatment. If they will not cooperate, doctors and schools can do precious little.

Children and medication. Children will vary in their ability to report that a medication has led to any changes, such as a sense of greater self-control or an ability to concentrate more. These changes, however, may be observed. For children, the greatest question usually is a social one. They worry about what their friends at school will think about their pill-taking. Slow-release medication that lasts the whole day can sometimes bypass this problem, if a particular prescription is available in that form.

Teenagers worry that they are still being treated

like children, having their parents hover over them to make sure they have taken their pills. Given the impulsive, often self-destructive nature of many teen-agers with these disorders, it is best that parents hold on to the medication. The best method for dispensing and taking the medication should be worked out between the child, parent, and therapist.

When children take medication, their behavioral change is often so dramatic that many people will notice. Let the child know that *he is the one who has begun to succeed*; it is not the pill that has had the success. Be sensitive to how you word your praise:

> WRONG WAY: Boy, those pills really work. Your grades have gotten so much better since you started taking them.

> RIGHT WAY: Your grades are much better now. Those pills let you show how smart you really are.

Seven Nagging Questions About Psychiatric Medications

1. *Don't they have terrible side effects?* Usually any side effects are mild and short-lived. Loss of appetite and poor sleep are the most common problems with stimulants. Most times, they fade quickly or can be controlled with other treatments, but it is extremely important that you keep your doctor informed of any unusual effects.

2. *Aren't these medicines a form of mind control?* Absolutely not! We tell children if they still want to hit a classmate, they will be able to. But if they do not want to hit a classmate, they will be able to keep themselves from doing so. Medications for disruptive disorders give children more control over themselves.

3. *Will the treatment turn my child into an addict?* This question has been extensively researched, and the answer is no. The findings are less surprising than one

might think on first glance. Many drug addicts began with youthful experimentation. A thirteen-year-old who has taken medication for six years knows far more about the experience of drugs than a typical classmate. Such children may know more about side effects and the difference between drugs that help and those that muddle the brain.

4. *Don't drugs prevent the development of moral responsibility?* Just the opposite. By letting your child take control of his actions, he can at last learn moral responsibility.

5. *Will the pills stifle my child's spontaneity and creativity?* No, they will give him control over it. The impulses and ideas persist, but the medication helps a child decide whether or not to act on those impulses.

6. *How about stifling social judgment?* As control over actions grows, children learn which actions are socially appropriate and which ones are not.

7. *Won't this medication teach the child to look for pills rather than solutions to problems?* A successful treatment plan uses more than medication. Long before his classmates, your child will learn the difference between problems that can be helped with medication and those that need other solutions.

Behavior Modification

Teaching your child a new way to behave does not have the dramatic results that come with medication, but can be an important part of a treatment plan. When a disruptive disorder persists, problems can develop that are not purely physical. A child who cannot act in the proper way does not learn the proper way of acting. Most families teach behavior by punishing bad actions; however, few things are better established in psychology than the fact that learning goes more easily and lasts longer by rewarding good actions. Punishment has its place in teaching children, but rewards should be your primary tool.

Some parents recoil from this idea. They ask why they should reward a child for doing what he should do anyway. We answer, "For the same reason you teach a child to walk before teaching him to run." In time your child will naturally act properly, but first you need to teach proper behavior.

Behavior modification treatment resembles medication in one important way: both require consistent and persistent effort from the parents. However, in other ways, behavior modification is more difficult—it takes more time, and the parents must be willing to devote real energy to the treatment. When properly undertaken, however, many parents find this part of the treatment particularly satisfying. Once they start the program, they discover how enjoyable giving praise is; they find that the treatment forces them to notice the many good things about their child. After such a long period of noticing only disruptive behavior, it is encouraging to see the good as well.

Rewards. The basic idea in behavior modification is simple: promote desirable behavior by immediately reinforcing the proper action. This order of teaching is most important. First comes the action, then comes the reinforcement.

WRONG WAY: You can watch television now if you promise to clean up your room right after.

RIGHT WAY: After you clean your room, you can watch television.

The wrong way provides the positive consequences before the action. The sequence of teaching should always be action *then* reinforcement. A promise to do something is not an action. If you find that you want a promise of future action, it is okay to promise a future reward in return, one that will follow the action. But do not give concrete rewards for words only.

Choosing rewards is an art. Do not make them

too expensive (a stereo set) or too fattening (candy kisses). One simple reward that makes good sense is the "rental" of household conveniences. Watching television, listening to the stereo, playing board games—all these are events that can be "rented." For example, a child can be rewarded with the right to watch another fifteen minutes of television. When evening comes, you can say, "Great, Brad, you have rented an hour and a half's worth of television time." With these rentals announce the reward at once, even though your child may not use the rental until a bit later. Once the rental is announced, do not go back on your word. We will discuss punishment a bit later.

One reward you should never offer is love. It is disastrous to say, "You did that so well, I love you much more now." The glue that holds a family together through these difficult times is the knowledge that the love is there no matter what. Keep your praise specific and focused on the child's learning: for example, saying "You did that homework so well, I am glad to see you are completing your assignments" points directly at the action you want to encourage.

Give praise often. This is the least expensive encouragement and the most welcome. Complicated tasks that require several steps may need repeated encouragement. Offer it gladly. If your child is going to help with a simple task like changing a light bulb in the ceiling lamp, offer praise when he brings the ladder, more encouragement as he holds the ladder steady, and still further thanks when he takes the bulb from your hand.

Punishments. Punishment has surprisingly little teaching value. Its one strength is that it puts a prompt halt to unacceptable activity. Use it to control immediate situations and use reward to direct your child's long-term development. Because punishment is so poor a teaching tool, severe penalties accomplish no more than moderate ones. Spankings may express anger; they teach nothing.

One method of punishment whose popularity has grown is the "timeout" system. It interrupts behavior and takes immediate charge of a situation. Designate some small area in your home as the timeout zone. Laundry rooms and bathrooms make good timeout areas, but make sure they are safe for the child to be in alone (and not too frightening for a young child). Playrooms and your child's room are usually poor choices, since they offer too many interesting distractions. The more boring the room the better. Explain to your child that punishment for intolerable behavior will be a timeout. When the child becomes too noisy or begins fighting with a brother or sister, call a timeout. The child must go to the timeout area and stay there quietly. The timeout does not have to be long. Five minutes is enough. Add a minute for each outburst that comes from the timeout area. Children quickly learn to be still during timeouts, but it does take some practice. Getting free of a timeout now becomes a reward for having been quiet for a few minutes.

Not every disturbance calls for a timeout. If you intervene early, you can prevent problems before they arise. Do not wait until small disturbances grow into large commotions. Step in and say *"Stop"* early on. Some parents hesitate because they feel they are always jumping on the child, never getting off his back. But parents who are also quick to praise and to congratulate find they are willing to intervene. They know they hand out both sides of the control. A good rule of thumb says that, at a minimum, praise twice as much as you criticize. Three times as much would not be excessive.

Techniques of behavioral modification do not produce immediate effects, but they force parents to think specifically about what their children are doing well and what they need to do better. Disruptive children are notorious for not responding immediately to the praise and punishments that govern their brothers and sisters so effectively. However, over time and as part of a general treatment plan, behavioral modification can contribute to the family's ability to control a disruptive disorder.

PART II

Attention-deficit Hyperactivity Disorder (ADHD)

CHAPTER 5

Living with ADHD

As we wrote earlier, youngsters with ADHD suffer from overactivity, inattention, and impulsivity inappropriate for their age. While these traits are common in all little children, the intensity of these behaviors, and their tendency to be exaggerated and to interfere with normal functioning, distinguish the **ADHD** child. It is these behaviors that can make living with **ADHD** so very difficult and exasperating.

These traits can be manifested in a variety of ways and will appear differently at various ages. The young child may appear to be overactive, always on the go, while the older child may only seem restless. The child may appear to have a hard time sitting still, or may constantly play with nearby objects.

Inattention may be revealed in problems completing homework, or in failure to finish activities. **ADHD** children are easily distracted, and parents often complain that the child does not listen to what they say. With peers, they may have trouble following the rules of games.

Impulsivity refers to the youngsters often acting before they think. In class, they may yell out the answers instead of waiting their turn. They may rush through their work, doing a sloppy job, not really paying attention to their task. Or they may inadvertently enter into dangerous situations, such as riding their bike down a dangerous street, without weighing the potential dangers to themselves.

A variety of features are associated with ADHD, including:

1. Emotional liability
2. Low frustration tolerance
3. Poor school performance
4. Poor peer relationships
5. Low self-esteem

These features also contribute to the difficulty of living with ADHD. Parents report that their child seems happy and content one moment, then dramatically changes for the worse over some seemingly inconsequential matter. Temper tantrums are common; the child has little ability to delay gratification.

ADHD children may be aggressive with siblings or their playmates to the point where their aggression appears to be a conduct disorder. In general, the aggression associated with ADHD, unlike that associated with conduct disorders, is not planned.

ADHD children may have difficulty in school because their disability interferes with their ability to conform to classroom rules. Also, as we will discuss later, some of these children may have learning disabilities, despite often having average or above-average intelligence.

All of these experiences of failure—in school, at

home, at play, and with their peers—help make the ADHD youngster feel different and unusual, even defective. Oftentimes, the child is understandably unhappy. This may be especially true if the child is intelligent but does poorly at school, and if the child's condition is undiagnosed. The child may ask himself, What's wrong with me, why am I so different? Usually, the child won't admit these feelings until he is much older. Often, the child becomes dejected and demoralized in his battle to live with ADHD, especially when it goes undetected.

The following cases demonstrate how difficult this can be, and how effective treatment can help the condition.

John's Story

When he was two weeks old, John was adopted. The agency reports that the birth was normal and the pregnancy showed no signs of anything out of the ordinary. The first signs of a problem appeared when John was three and began nursery school. The teacher told his parents that John was not able to sit still and sometimes defied her instructions. His classmates liked him, but sometimes he was too aggressive; when overstimulated he could become wild. The condition did not change when John turned four, and after his second year his teachers recommended that he stay in nursery school and not progress to kindergarten because of his "immaturity." Job requirements, however, forced the family to move, and John did start kindergarten in a new school. His new teacher reported that John was loud, always active, inattentive, and could be very silly. His new classmates did not seem to like him much, for John often got into shouting and shoving matches. He did not appear to function well in the school environment, either academically or socially. At home, too, his parents noticed that he had become more argumentative, ignoring instructions until after they had been repeated many times.

At this point his parents brought him to us for examination, and we diagnosed ADHD. Given his level of dysfunction, we decided that medication was indicated. The drug of choice in cases like this is a psychostimulant, such as Ritalin, Dexedrine, or Cylert; in this case Ritalin was selected, and it had an immediate effect. John became much more cooperative, both at school and at home, and he seemed to grow happier as he saw himself take charge of his actions. After a few months of daily medication, we changed the regimen, limiting him to Ritalin on school days. On weekends and holidays he did not need the drug. Along with the medication, we had recommended individual therapy to help John build up his self-esteem and social skills, and counseling for John's parents. After several months, the therapist decreased John's weekly sessions to once-a-month meetings. During the school year, John takes the same dose of Ritalin, and, we are happy to report, he continues to do well.

Steven's Story

Steven is an active teenager. He was an active school child, an active nursery school boy, an active toddler, active infant, and, indeed, an active fetus. His mother remembers thinking she "was carrying a football team." She knew by the time he was seven weeks old that something was wrong, because Steven was never at peace. At seven months Steven had to wear a cast on his left foot to correct an orthopedic problem, yet he would still crawl all over the house and once managed to wriggle his foot out of the cast. Nothing in the home seemed beyond his reach or curiosity. He poured laundry detergent and stained his mother's valuable coat; he hurled food against every conceivable item in the kitchen; and when he was three years old, he spent a night in the hospital after eating the family dog's medicine. If left alone for ninety seconds he could open the front door and get halfway down the block.

When he was three he entered nursery school, where teachers promptly reported that he was too active, had a short attention span, and was having trouble making friends because he was so aggressive. He hit, and once even bit, classmates who got in his way. When he was four, the school recommended that the family seek professional help for Steven. They went to a psychologist, who taught the parents how to follow a more consistent and thoughtful approach to disciplining Steven. Before these sessions his father had felt that Steven needed to be taken firmly in hand and not be allowed to get away with things. His mother thought that Steven was criticized too harshly for doing childish things. Steven's activity level did not decline after the parents' counseling sessions, but Steven did reduce his aggressive behavior.

A crisis came when Steven reached second grade. His teacher complained that he was disruptive. He was not particularly aggressive or defiant, but he served as the "class clown," emitting a steady stream of noises and actions that distracted his classmates. His work was sloppy, suggesting no effort beyond a rush to completion. He often forgot to take books home for schoolwork, and when he did remember them, homework was agony. His parents had to spend hours sitting with him, trying to get him to do the assignment. At home his one interest appeared to be video games. He picked many fights with his sister. He was especially irritable in the morning. He complained about getting dressed, about brushing his teeth, and about the rush to get ready for school. He had to be reminded several times to take his work with him, and even then a check just as he was leaving often found he had forgotten his books, papers, or both. It was at this point that his parents decided to see a psychiatrist.

Our examination led to a diagnosis of ADHD, and we prescribed a Ritalin trial, individual therapy for Steven, and counseling for the parents. We also recommended examination by a learning dis abilities specialist, to see if Steven had any prob lems in that area. Testing put Steven's IQ in th superior range, but he did have poor motor skill that interfered with his handwriting. He also ha poor organizational skills. The learning specialis recommended special help in school to work o these learning difficulties.

At first we introduced Ritalin on a twice-a-da basis (morning and lunchtime). The effect on schoo behavior was soon apparent. Steven was less fidget less the class clown, and more attentive, but at hom he continued to have problems. Homework continued to be an ordeal; he remained restless and he regular ly got into fights with his sister. We added a lat afternoon dose of Ritalin to his prescription, and th effect was dramatic. His behavior improved at home and he was much less irritable in the mornings. Hi schoolwork, however, continued to be disappointing It only improved noticeably at the start of the nex school year, when he transferred to a private schoo with far fewer students per class. His grades im proved, although they were still not reflecting hi ability, and even the homework sessions seemed les like a battle.

A few years later Steven's behavior at schoo declined. The familiar symptoms of impulsive, silly and unfocused behavior increased markedly. Steven' father had undergone cardiac surgery, and the inci dent had been very stressful for the whole family Steven had become increasingly anxious. At first we thought that talking about his feelings in therapy would best help Steven, but when this approach had no effect, we increased the Ritalin dosage and Steven returned to his more controlled behavior. His school work remained uneven. Sometimes he got As, some times Fs. But when he entered high school, he showed a marked improvement. Now his grades were As and Bs.

During summer vacations we tried to take Steven

off Ritalin, but the attempt failed. Without medication Steven became overactive and quarrelsome, even
in the unstructured environment of a summer break.
At first he showed no sensitivity to the effects his
unmedicated behavior had on himself, his parents,
and his sister. He would pester his sister until she
reacted, and then said the ensuing uproar was all her
fault. But slowly the many counseling sessions did
help him get a better understanding of his role in the
battles around him. His newfound success in high
school came when he began to apply himself seriously, and that change, too, may have come from counseling. He has become a popular boy and now shows
no antisocial tendencies.

These two cases show us much about the experience of living with an Attention-deficit Hyperactivity
Disorder. Steven's story in particular shows many of
the features that have led us to believe that ADHD is
a natural handicap, much like being born with a
weakened leg or arm. When the problem is physical,
however, parents are usually able to accept the idea
that treatment is going to take more than moral
fortitude and a good pep talk. Psychiatric handicaps
are not always accepted with the same understanding. In Steven's case, we can see that he was born
overactive. In our experience, it is not uncommon for
a mother to comment that the baby was very active
in the uterus. Steven's mother's remark that she
knew something was wrong when he was only seven
weeks old is not surprising. About a third of ADHD
mothers remark on difficulties in the first year. Many
parents say that once their child began to walk, the
toddler was "always on the go." Or they say that "he
didn't walk—he ran." The story about being able to
open the front door and dash down the block is one
we have heard more than once.

The first crisis commonly comes at nursery school.
Parents may dismiss difficult behavior in a one- or
two-year-old, but when a child turns three, many

parents realize that something more is going on than an unusually trying case of the "terrible twos." Three year-olds make a great transition. Their language develops dramatically, and their social skills advance in leaps and bounds. This is the point at which the parents of an ADHD child often experience the first public rejection of their baby. We saw in John's case that this criticism is not absolute. A teacher may report, "At times he acts like he has ants in his pants" but it is nothing major." Other times, however, teachers complain that a youngster cannot be still. The parents of classmates may even refuse to let the child come over for a visit.

Free play at preschool often has a random quality. Ordinary children and ADHD children are not easily distinguished in these settings, but when it comes time to sit still and listen to the teacher tell a story, the difference can be apparent. ADHD children do not easily sit quietly through something their classmates may enjoy. Their classmates begin to object and reject the ADHD child. Already by age seven, many of these children show reduced self-esteem. At home, if a child is not unbearably difficult, parents may not realize how active their child is, especially if they are not familiar with typical behavior at different ages. Therefore, some parents do not realize that the child has a disorder until he enters school.

The first treatment tried in Steven's case was parental counseling, a common approach for a case like his. A few studies indicate medication like Ritalin may be helpful to some youngsters even at this early age, but the results are less predictable than in older children. Besides, medication may be necessary for many years, so with young children we like to stay away from medication at first, if possible, and begin with a treatment that focuses more on changing the environment. In fact, environmental manipulation is always attempted with ADHD youngsters at any age. It may be especially

effective in preschool children, since they don't
have the same pressure to conform in the classroom that older, school-age children have. Environmental manipulation may be all that's necessary
for the younger child. In Steven's case, the counseling helped reduce his aggression. A decade later, as
a teenager, both he and society still benefit from
that early control over aggression. His teachers
may not have been delighted to see him channel his
restlessness into being a "class clown," but it was
much better than being the class bully.

The major change in parenting methods brought
about by the therapy sessions was the introduction of
a more consistent approach to rewards and punishment. Many parents complain that their child does
not respond either to rewards or to punishments. The
observation is so widespread that it has even been
proposed that the primary problem of ADHD children is a poor ability to learn from a system of
rewards and punishments. This is an interesting idea,
for psychology has firmly established that any crea-
ture with a backbone can learn from reinforcements
(the technical term for rewards and punishments).
Many psychologists deny that reinforcement training
is the key to all human learning, but all of them do
agree that reinforcement is responsible for some learning. A discovery that ADHD children cannot learn
this way would be surprising indeed. However, there
is some evidence that the problem is just the opposite and that ADHD children seem so sensitive to
rewards and punishments that they are unusually
confused by any inconsistencies in reinforcement
training.

It is very important for parents, especially of
ADHD youngsters to deal with their youngsters in a
consistent manner. The differences between two parents' styles of discipline, something found in every
family, is especially disturbing to ADHD children.

Most ADHD children first see a doctor about
their behavior when they enter school, especially

during the first three grades. Sometimes a child is so intelligent that it is only in the fourth or fifth grades that his marks begin to suffer. Usually, the crisis comes sooner. The second grade seems to be an especially difficult year for hyperactive youngsters. By then the teacher knows the problem is not just one of adaptation to school, and the classroom demands step up a notch or two. Steven came in for a full evaluation during his second grade.

Steven's homework ordeal is another common feature of the ADHD school experience. Parents often tell us that to get through homework, they have to sit right there and keep the child's attention focused on the work. One-on-one relations commonly work much better than group settings. That is why parents are often astonished by a teacher's report of the child's learning difficulties. At home, working with a parent, the child comprehends lessons quickly and easily. But at school, with all of its distractions, his problem surfaces.

Steven's ability to play video games is another detail we often see. Other parents will say that their ADHD child can sit still for hours watching certain television programs, or he can spend a day happily fishing with Dad, showing excellent concentration during the outing. It's not that the child can never be attentive—he can keep focused if the activity is interesting enough.

Sometimes youngsters display variable degrees of difficulties. Take the story of Mark. His early years showed no signs of trouble, and he did not come to us until the third grade; however, his kindergarten, first-grade, and second-grade teachers had commented that he was restless, very social and loved to talk. When he could be silenced, he often seemed to dream off to a world of his own. After a thorough evaluation, we diagnosed him as having ADHD. Mark, like some other ADHD children, appeared to have a "hyperactive mouth." Parents of these children will say, "He can just talk and talk and talk and talk and talk and talk." And sometimes the children have hyperactive imaginations, too. They may tell some very tall tales. During psychiatric evaluation, these children will often respond with elaborate discussions of fantasies that other youngsters will not share (such as seeing a ghost). Usually these fantasies are not psychotic—merely an indication of a very imaginative child.

At the school-age level, we are more inclined to include a medication like Ritalin in the treatment of ADHD. Both John's and Steven's cases illustrate successful medication therapy. Maintaining children on a drug requires steady monitoring, and one hopes for the experience John had, but Steven's experience is not unusual and nothing to worry about. Even before coming to us, John's difficulties were much greater at school than at home, so it is not surprising that he did not need medication for home living. The family stress following Steven's father's heart problems may have been a "red herring," and probably coincided with Steven having developed a tolerance to Ritalin—requiring a higher dosage for the drug to continue to be effective.

The changes Steven showed in high school were important and encouraging. It used to be said that "hyperactivity" simply faded away during the teenage years. ADHD, however, comprises a cluster of different manifestations at different ages. It is true that overactivity ceases to be a common complaint about ADHD teenagers, but the impulsivity and inattention can persist. For some ADHD youngsters, the impulsivity, low frustration levels, and possible oppositional tendencies can lead to increased concern about "rebelliousness." Adolescence does have a potential for conflict and turmoil, but the average teenager in the average family gets through the period without tremendous chaos and turmoil. Psychology has come to understand, the James Dean "Rebel Without a Cause" image does not represent the typical teenager. The rebelliousness of many ADHD teen-

agers can be seen as a symptom of continuing difficulties. This rebelliousness sometimes takes a seriously
antisocial turn. We will discuss that development in
Part III. Steven, however, responded to adolescence
by knuckling down to his work. At last his grades
began to reflect his intelligence. Partly this result
reflected how hard his parents had worked to help
him. Partly it reflected his own intelligence. As he
matured, he realized that, if he wanted to participate
fully in life, he had to do well in school. Instead of
becoming a rebellious or conduct disordered boy,
Steven has grown into a socially adept and academically successful young man.

CHAPTER 6

Educating Children with ADHD

In the schoolroom, ADHD turns up everywhere. Peace Corps volunteers returning from remote village schools will say, "Oh, yes. I remember a student with those symptoms." The formal rules, the demand for prolonged attention, and the standardized expectations that a teacher brings to a classroom seem designed deliberately to catch up the ADHD child. Realistically, there is no way to survive in the modern world without an education. A bright child who is unable to adapt to the rules of the classroom is at a greater disadvantage than the equally bright classmate on crutches.

Adding to the difficulty is the increased risk of a learning disability. Learning problems are more common among ADHD children than with ordinary children. Our clinical experience has been that attention-deficit hyperactivity and learning disabilities can complicate and partially mask each other. Sometimes a diagnosis will catch one part of the problem and miss the other. Whenever we hear about a child who underachieves at school, we consider a learning disability, even though it may be apparent that much of the difficulty can be explained by an attention-deficit hyperactivity disorder.

Marla's Story

Marla was brought to us for psychiatric evaluation when she was in the third grade. During her first years she had shown some language delay, but frequent ear infections may have contributed to that problem. She was not an especially active child, but in nursery school her teachers reported that Marla enjoyed playing with her peers. During structured time, such as story time, it was not easy to hold her interest, and she had to be given directions repeatedly. Her mother had noticed this same behavior at home. When she began school, Marla was discovered to have a mild learning disability. In school, she was likable, without major behavioral problems. She was mildly disruptive, however—too social, too fidgety, too talkative, too involved with her peers. Even with her learning disability she did not seem to be performing up to her level. She did not complete her tasks, did not organize her efforts well, and showed some anxiety about doing schoolwork. She was sent to us to see if she might have an emotional problem that was impeding her performance. We found that she had an ADHD. She was far less temperamental than is typical for ADHD boys, but her overactivity showed itself in her fidgety behavior and sociability. We prescribed Ritalin, and it helped, but the treatment also included educational counseling. Her parents were advised to get Marla involved in nonacademic activities. This part of the treatment succeeded, and Marla's self-esteem improved.

Diagnosing Marla's ADHD was probably more difficult because she was a girl. A girl's hyperactivity is often less aggravating than a boy's. Since ADHD is generally more common in boys than in girls (a 4–9:1 male:female ratio), there is a great temptation to see ADHD as only a boy's problem. Why ADHD is seen more in boys than in girls is not known. Interestingly, a variety of central nervous system problems, such as mental retardation and learning disabilities, are more common in prepubertal boys than girls.

ADHD appears to run in families. Studies indicate that in as many as 20–30 percent of these youngsters, there is a family member (parent or sibling) who acted similarly in childhood. It's not uncommon for mothers to tell us that their in-laws have said, "Johnny's dad was just the same way when he was little." Also noted in families of ADHD children is a higher than average incidence of alcohol dependence or abuse, antisocial personality disorder, hysteria, learning problems, and possibly mood and anxiety disorders.

In particularly difficult cases, where the parent-child relationship is particularly negative, it may be necessary for the ADHD child to attend a specialized boarding school for youngsters with emotional and learning disabilities. These schools offer small classes and can use a variety of techniques (such as behavioral modification and group therapy) that can enable children with problems to grow in a positive fashion. But these residential schools are recommended only after other treatments have been tried. Most ADHD children can continue within their normal school setting, although they may need extra help. Their success is facilitated if:

- The teachers understand that the child's behavior reflects a disorder, not necessarily a bad attitude.
- The teachers help by encouraging the child at least as much as they criticize and punish.
- The school cooperates in any program of medication treatment.

• The teachers respect the child's privacy, and do not let other students or their parents know of the ADHD diagnosis.

Our experience indicates teachers are quite sensitive to these issues, but we recommend that the parents share their concerns with the teacher. Encourage teachers to take a special interest in your child. Teachers will often ask for our advice on how they can help a youngster to learn more effectively. Ask the teacher for suggestions about what *you* can do—a question like, "I wonder if you have noticed anything that has particularly caught my child's fancy. If you have, I might be able to encourage that interest at home." Perhaps the teacher has noticed something, perhaps not. But now that the issue has been raised, the teacher may become more interested and alert.

The following recommendations are for teachers who work with ADHD youngsters. They are taken from a special booklet for teachers written by the parents' support group C.H.A.D.D. (Parents of Children with Attention Deficit Disorder).

TEACHERS AND ADHD*

Giving Instructions to Students

1. Maintain eye contact with the ADD student during verbal instruction.
2. Make directions clear and concise. Be consistent with daily instructions.
3. Simplify complex directions. Avoid multiple commands.
4. Make sure ADD student comprehends task before beginning it.
5. Repeat in a calm, positive manner, if needed.

---

*Recommendations reprinted with appreciation to C.H.A.D.D. National Offices.

6. Help ADD child to feel comfortable with seeking assistance (most ADD children won't ask).
7. Gradually reduce assistance. ADD children need more help for a longer period of time than the average child.
8. Require a daily assignment notebook if necessary.

   • Make sure student writes down all assignments correctly each day. If the student is not capable of this then the teacher should help the student.
   • Parents and teachers should sign notebook daily to signify completion of homework assignments.
   • Parents and teachers may use notebook for daily communication with each other.

Helping Students Perform Assignments

1. Give out only one task at a time.
2. Monitor frequently. Use a supportive attitude.
3. Modify assignments as needed. Consult with Special Education personnel to determine specific strengths and weaknesses of the student. Develop an individualized educational program.
4. Make sure you are testing knowledge and not attention span.
5. Give extra time for certain tasks. The ADD student may work more slowly. Don't penalize for needed extra time.
6. Keep in mind that ADD children are easily frustrated. Stress, pressure and fatigue can break down the ADD child's self-control and lead to poor behavior.

Behavior Modification and Self-Esteem Enhancement: Providing Supervision and Discipline

1. Remain calm, state infraction of rule, and don't debate or argue with student.
2. Have pre-established consequences for misbehavior.
3. Administer consequences immediately and monitor proper behavior frequently.

4. Enforce rules of the classroom consistently.
5. Make sure discipline is appropriate and "fits the crime" without being overly harsh.
6. Avoid ridicule and criticism. Remember, ADD children have difficulty staying in control.
7. Avoid *publicly* reminding students on medication to take their medicine.

ONE-ON-ONE LEARNING

All children enjoy "hands on" learning more than they like sitting at a desk and hearing about something, and this principle is especially true for ADHD children. Children with ADHD also do best when they work one-on-one with an adult instead of in a group setting. Parents can combine this hands-on idea with a one-on-one approach to encourage their child to develop interests, experiences, and self-confidence. Some typical projects include:

Science collections. Collections can be great fun for the wandering eye. There is plenty to distract and keep a child amused, yet a general organized theme remains. A collection can be as simple as saving plastic bottles. You will be surprised to discover how many different sorts of plastics and shapes you find in no time. You and your child can build your own museum to display the collection, and both of you can invent experiments to discover new details about plastic. What happens if plastic freezes? How much weight can a grocery store's plastic bag hold before it rips? Can you find a way to break an "unbreakable" plastic bottle?

Reading together. Most educators believe strongly that the best way to make a child a reader is to begin reading aloud on a regular, or even daily, basis when the child is one or two years old. This idea may be abandoned early on with an ADHD child, who refuses to sit through a story. Try again, only this time have your child tell you part of the story. Look at the pictures in a picture book and imagine what the story says. Action figures and toys can also serve as imaginative triggers to start a story going. You can tell part of a story yourself.

Hands-on math. Few things are more abstract than the mathematics taught in schools. Help your child see that arithmetic is real. Play counting games or do magic (addition or subtraction) with household items. Make math fun.

Hands-on art. Do not forget the arts. Your child may find great delight in dance, in clay, in music, and in painting. A child with skill in these areas has much to offer society. Working one-on-one in this area depends partly on your own abilities and interests, but if you love dance, do not assume your ADHD child cannot share your taste. Give it a try.

Physical skills. Children value playing. They judge their friends and themselves by how well they play. Many ADHD children think less well of themselves because their impulsiveness, poor concentration, and sometimes mild motor or movement problems make them clumsy athletes, but there are so many games these days that your child will probably be good at some of them. Medication may help a child play in a more focused, active way, instead of just being wildly energetic. Children often suffer great loss of self-esteem before their ADHD is diagnosed. Finding a good sport at which the child can succeed—soccer, sprinting, swimming—can be an important tool in rebuilding confidence.

Social skills. You cannot do everything: your child will always see you as a parent, not a peer. All children need good friends as well as good parents. Many ADHD children have terrible social relationships when they come to us. They have been rejected too often. Moving to new neighborhoods or new schools does not always help. Other children may quickly reject the new ADHD child. Once treatment has begun, your child may be able to act more acceptably, but still not know many social skills. Years of rejection do take their toll. If your child's social position does not improve, you can help by finding one good friend. It can be someone at school who gets along with your child, or the slightly older (and more mature) friend of an older sibling, or a relative, or it can be another ADHD child who has been diagnosed and is now being treated. Remember, if your child has a tendency to be overly excited easily, and is stubborn and aggressive, don't encourage a friendship with someone with similar difficulties. This will only serve to reinforce your youngster's negative patterns and probably help him learn new ones. Wherever you find this suitable child, he or she must be found. Encourage the friendship. Arrange times for them to get together. Take them to movies together. Organize their social lives until they start to do it themselves. When we see a child who has begun to make friends, we begin to believe he is on the road to success.

CHAPTER 7

Treating ADHD

The cause or causes of ADHD remains unknown. Investigators continue to search for some abnormality—a malfunction in the brain—but a specific neurologic abnormality remains unidentified. It may be that there is not one cause, but a variety of factors that create the symptoms of ADHD.

Although the neurological and biological abnormalities in ADHD youngsters are still being evaluated, it is clear that medication can play a major role in the treatment of this disorder.

Recent studies have tried to identify a physical cause for ADHD. Many of these studies have centered upon levels of neurotransmitters—chemicals that act as messengers between nerve cells and are believed to affect a wide range of emotions and behaviors. The medications commonly used to treat hyperactivity do affect levels of neurotransmitters; however, the exact process of how these medications work is unknown.

An exciting study was done recently by researchers at the National Institute of Mental Health using a fairly new brain imaging technique known as Positron Emission Tomography scanning. The researchers found that brain's ability to metabolize glucose was 8 percent lower in adults who had histories of childhood hyperactivity and continued to have symptoms into adulthood, than those of a comparably normal group of adults. Each of the adults with reduced glucose metabolism was also the natural parent of a hyperactive child. The largest reductions of glucose metabolism were found in two areas of the brain that are involved in control of attention and motor activity. Therefore, the concrete link between ADHD and cerebral dysfunction is beginning to be identified. It is hoped that further research will result in even more effective medications.

Currently, the major class of drugs used to treat ADHD in youngsters are stimulants, with an estimated 200,000 to 400,000 children in the United States taking stimulants for attention and behavioral problems. These stimulant medications do not overexcite the hyperactive child—rather they help the child to concentrate better and be less physically restless. The effectiveness of stimulants was first demonstrated in the 1930s, but at that time psychiatry's therapeutic emphasis lay in treating unconscious conflicts, and not a great deal was done with the finding that an amphetamine called Benzedrine improved children's behavior in school. During the 1950s, interest in psychopharmacology began to grow. In 1959, the first reports of using methylphenidate (brand name: Ritalin) in hyperactive children occurred. Since that time, many studies have been done using stimulants like methylphenidate and dextroamphetamine (Dexedrine) in ADHD. Originally, stimulant treatment was erroneously thought to be less necessary and fraught with problems in adolescent children. We now know that ADHD teenagers continue to respond well to stimulants. For this reason, medication therapy is often continued into adolescence and even into adulthood.

A continuing question about any medication, especially one as powerful as a stimulant, concerns dosage. In general, we recommend the smallest dose needed to have the desired effect. But at the same time, it is important not to underprescribe a medication. Often a child whose condition is classified "unresponsive" to a stimulant has just not received the proper dose. A physician needs to adjust the dosage according to the patient's responsiveness and side effects.

In explaining to the child why he is taking the medication, it needs to be made clear that the medication can help him sit still and pay attention, but he can still be disruptive if he wants to. In this way we try to reinforce to the child that he is in control of his own behavior.

RITALIN

Methylphenidate, or, as it is best known, Ritalin, is the most commonly prescribed stimulant in the United States. About 75 percent of ADHD children respond favorably to it. Some of the more frequent side effects are disturbed sleep and loss of appetite; both are typical responses to a stimulant. These effects are often transient, or can be modified by a change in dosage, and therefore may not require a cessation of medication. An important possible long-term side effect is slowing of growth in height and/or weight. Studies are conflicting in this issue of how often this side effect occurs and how significant it is. Therefore we recommend that prescribing physicians should monitor growth in height and weight. Other potential side effects include headache, stomachache, rapid heartbeat, changes in blood pressure, dizziness. In rare instances, Ritalin may cause a drug-related psychosis (a "break" from reality) or a movement problem. Children with a history of a tic disorder, or a family history of Tourette's syndrome, should not receive Ritalin, since the drug may precipitate these conditions. Because of the risk of any side effects—no matter how rare—family members should report to their doctor immediately any unusual side effects. Similarly, the physician should monitor the patient carefully for any side effects. We realize that these potential side effects may make some parents wary of medication. We must stress that all medications—even aspirin—have potentially serious side effects. Stimulant medications are the most studied medications used by child psychiatrists and are generally the most benign. Serious side effects in children are very rare.

Because Ritalin is a controlled substance, certain practices must be observed in writing a prescription. However, these practices should not alarm parents, since the abuse of Ritalin by ADHD children is virtually unknown. The medication fosters control over their actions, but does not produce a pleasurable "high."

The popularity of Ritalin derives from its combination of important benefits with minimal side effects. Some of the more flamboyant critics of medication accuse teachers and parents of "turning their children into zombies, just to quiet them down." But Ritalin, when properly prescribed, should not turn children into zombies. Some children, but *not* the majority, may appear to be slower. If this occurs, either a lower dosage or different medication may be required. Most youngsters, however, should still be able to romp actively and energetically on the playground. Indeed the only before-

and-after effect likely to be noticed in play is that the ADHD child may have become a better athlete when playing with peers. The zest and excitement is still there as it always was, but now the actions are less scattered and more focused. A child on Ritalin is not a "changed person" in the sense that old virtues have been suppressed or erased. Enthusiasms persist, but now your child has taken control of behavior, at last letting the true child emerge from behind the barricade of uncontrollable feelings.

Ritalin's effects are short-lived, which is why a prescription usually calls for taking medication a few times a day. Commonly, it is taken with or right after breakfast and right before or after school lunch. Because Ritalin's effects are short-lived, parents or teachers may notice the return of the ADHD symptoms (such as irritability and increased energy) in the late afternoon. If this occurs, a late afternoon dosage of the drug may be required.

A timed-release form of the drug may allow the child to function well the whole day on a single pill. But this timed-release alternative is available in only one dosage, so it may not be appropriate for many children.

Sometimes a combination of Ritalin and other medications is prescribed, depending on the nature of the youngster's difficulties. In general, however, Ritalin by itself serves well over the long term.

Usually a child taking an effective dose of Ritalin improves at school. Behavior in class is better, and attention improves as well, but Ritalin does not make a child smarter. Perception, insights, and goal-directed activities all seem much better, and each development is probably the result of improved attention span. Do not expect Ritalin by itself to make up for whatever your child has already missed in school, and it definitely will not help with any specific learning disabilities. Besides Ritalin, a treatment program for ADHD should include specific steps aimed at helping a child regain his academic footing.

Treatment programs also should include efforts to help the home environment. No matter how well disposed the parents are toward helping their handicapped child, the disorder usually disrupts the household and the family needs some guidance in regaining its balance. But even a loving and supportive home may not be enough. Even a child coming from the most positive environment may still need medication. This statement would not surprise anyone facing an obviously physical disorder. If a child has poor eyesight, we know that a good family is still important, but eyeglasses are also a must. Without them, such a child is much less likely to become an independent being, no matter how loving the home. ADHD is the same: Medication and a good home environment get a child up to life's starting line.

OTHER MEDICATIONS

Ritalin is usually the first drug prescribed for a child diagnosed with ADHD, but sometimes a particular child proves unresponsive, even when dosage is increased and given adequate time, or there may be medical reasons that preclude its use. In these cases, a variety of other medications may be prescribed.

Dexedrine

Dextroamphetamine sulfate (better known by the brand name Dexedrine) has the longest history of use, and it is often the first alternative tried after considering Ritalin. It is available in short-acting and in slow-release form. It may have a stronger effect than Ritalin in reducing appetite, but that effect is not certain in any particular child. Although longer lasting than Ritalin, its anti-ADHD effects are still short-lived, necessitating more than one dose a day. Potential side effects to Dexedrine are similar to Ritalin.

Cylert

Another commonly used medication is magnesium pemoline (brand name: Cylert). Its greatest drawback is the long time it takes to achieve its effects (about three weeks). Its strength is the long-lasting effect of a single dose. The once-a-day dose makes Cylert particularly attractive in cases in which taking medication at school is a problem. It is also a popular choice in cases where the side effects of Ritalin and Dexedrine prove unmanageable. Potential side effects are similar to the other stimulants, but also may include liver abnormalities. For this reason, periodic liver function tests should be administered.

Tricyclic Antidepressants (TCAs)

Tricyclic antidepressants are sometimes given in ADHD cases if stimulants do not work or cannot be used. If we are treating a teenager, who may also be a substance abuser, the use of TCAs may be preferred, since these drugs are less likely than the stimulants to be abused. In ADHD treatment, the most commonly used TCAs are imipramine and desipramine. Potential side effects include: sedation, dry mouth, dizziness, constipation, increased heart rate, changes in blood pressure, and heart conduction problems. Because of potential cardiac effects, an electrocardiogram (EKG) and blood tests are necessary to monitor the medication's side effects.

Neuroleptics

Occasionally, neuroleptic medications such as thioridazine (Mellaril) are used to treat ADHD. These drugs are not usually the medications of first choice, but they may be necessary in treating difficult cases, especially if the youngster exhibits out-of-control aggression. In such cases, they can be quite helpful. If used, we strive to limit the duration of therapy, since they can potentially interfere with the child's cognitive function, and can cause tardive dyskinesia, a potentially permanent movement disorder. Other potential side effects include: restlessness, sedation, liver, blood, and gastrointestinal effects.

Another medication, *lithium*, does not appear to have a role in the treatment of ADHD, unless aggressive behavior, or a concomitant mood disorder is also present. In addition, if the child shows aggressive behavior, some of the other medications described in the Conduct Disorder sections may be used.

OTHER TREATMENTS

Individual Therapy

This can be helpful for the youngster's difficulties with impulsivity, low self-esteem, and poor peer relationships. ADHD children need to learn to think before they act and recognize the consequences of their behavior. Often attempts at insightful psychotherapy can be difficult and unproductive with ADHD children, since these children are more focused on the here and now and have difficulty gaining insight into their behavior and waiting for the long-term results of psychotherapy. A medication may have the added bonus of enhancing psychotherapy by allowing the child to concentrate better. One therapeutic technique used with these children is Virginia Douglas's "Stop, look, and listen" method. This method attempts to teach children how to retrain their attention and hopefully be less impulsive.

Family Therapy

Family therapy may involve all the family members, or at times may refer to sessions for parental counseling. Family therapy is a way of opening up parent-child communications. Sometimes, after years of difficulties, families have developed patterns that reinforce negative behaviors in all members. Patterns that can be difficult to change.

In family therapy, parents are taught to work on consistent methods of limit setting. A hyperactive child can test a parent's resources every minute. A parent often needs help in learning when to ignore certain behaviors. Work is done to educate the parents on the nature of their child's difficulties. The message to parents is that their youngsters may have difficulties but they still need to learn to be responsible individuals, although they may need extra help. The message to the child is that despite his having some extra difficulty which may take extra effort to overcome, in the end he is responsible for his own actions.

Behavior Modification

Behavioral modification is often used to help modify the negative behaviors that ADHD youngsters may display. Often this modification may be done through the use of "star charts" in younger children, and behavioral contracts with the older children. The principles of this treatment approach have been discussed in Chapter 4. Behavior modification appear to work best when children are also taking medication.

The Feingold Diet

Dr. Benjamin Feingold, an allergist, proposed that hyperactivity is a response to food additives in the diet, and that it could be controlled by eliminating foods that contain things like artificial colors and additives. The Feingold diet probably peaked in 1982, when the National Institutes of Health organized a three-day conference on "Defined Diets and Hyperactivity." The studies presented there did not find that the diet resulted in improvement of the symptoms of ADHD children. In our practice, we have had some parents come to us and claim that the diet has worked to some degree for their youngsters. Often they complain that the diet is very hard to follow, especially since it makes their child feel different from his peers. Some psychiatrists feel it is the amount of attention and effort the family puts into maintaining the diet that actually accounts for any success the diet may have.

In summary, it appears that dietary modification may help some hyperactive children, but it does not work for the majority of youngsters.

Treating ADHD always begins with uncertainty. How severe is it? How responsive will a child be to a particular medication? How many other forms of treatment will be needed in addition to the medication? Only experience will tell. Keeping the condition under control requires being able to adjust to changing circumstances and responses.

Another uncertainty is the family. How strong will the parents be? A diagnosis of ADHD means that the parents must work twice as hard as ordinary parents, and this same struggle applies equally to the child. The success of raising any handicapped child depends mightily on the confident love of the parents. The best results are achieved when the parent and child work closely together.

PART III

Conduct Disorder

CHAPTER 8

What Conduct Disorder Is

The medical phrase "conduct disorder" is so nonjudgmental as to sound harmless. Many people can recall a time or two when a teacher said their conduct had better improve, but a conduct disorder (CD) is not simply a tendency to become unruly and to act up. The behavior of the children and teenagers who suffer from it is so routinely antisocial that it gets in the way of their everyday lives. This antisocial behavior may be characterized by constant fighting, drug abuse, vandalism, and excessive risk-taking. Classwork, social activity, and family life can be in a state of disarray because of this antisocial behavior. Some CD children become antisocial for shrewd, if devious, reasons, as a means to money or status. Other children are antisocial because, as with other disruptive disorders, they are impulsive and out of control.

One of the greatest fears about a disruptive disorder is that it will take on antisocial complications.

Children with ADHD are at risk for developing a conduct disorder, but being at risk is not the same as being doomed. We believe that the sooner a disruptive disorder is diagnosed and treated, the less likely it is to become an antisocial disorder.

American psychiatry recognizes two forms of antisocially disruptive disorders. One, known as Oppositional Defiant Disorder (see Chapter 3 for the diagnostic criteria), is the less serious form: A child may simply refuse to obey rules or instructions. The other, Conduct Disorder (see Chapter 3 for the diagnostic criteria), shows, as the DSM-III-R bluntly puts it, a persistent pattern of conduct in which "the basic rights of others and . . . society norms or rules are violated." Conduct-disordered children may behave so callously that they seem not to care for the feelings, happiness, and hopes of others. They show little or no guilt or regret for either their actions or the consequences. Conduct-disordered children can also turn against themselves. Suicide, attempted suicides, and threats of suicide are recurring complicating features of this disorder.

The difference between oppositional and conduct-disordered children may in part depend on age, and in part on sex. Conduct disorders lead to openly antisocial acts, such as crime and violence, and boys—especially older boys—tend more toward these external forms of self-expression. Estimates of the ratio of conduct-disordered boys to similarly affected girls vary, but are in the range of about nine boys for every two girls. Girls and younger boys tend more toward internalized symptoms. Girls are more likely to engage in self-defeating and defiant behaviors, such as promiscuity, rather than to be aggressive and dangerous. This may make a girl less likely to come to professional attention. A boy's antisocial behavior is often serious enough to force people to pay attention. A girl's behavior often leads to promiscuity and running away rather than to trouble with the law.

Whether their actions are aggressive toward othrs or directed against themselves, antisocial children do share certain traits. They emphasize short-erm gains and give little thought to tomorrow. They re less able than their peers to get along with people their own age. They are also less responsive han normal children to social approval or disapproval. This last trait makes behavioral modification programs more difficult than they otherwise would be. However, although conduct-disordered children re not deeply moved by praise or condemnation, hey respond normally when they receive more concrete rewards, such as ice cream or extra television ime.

The following case studies have been drawn from ur clinical experience to illustrate the way children who are suspected of conduct disorder can be treated when a sound additional diagnosis can be made.

CONDUCT DISORDER OR ATTENTION DEFICIT?

Anne was a fifteen-year-old student in the tenth grade, he youngest of three sisters in an upper-middle-class amily with high educational and economic attainments. Anne's oldest sister was a junior at an Ivy League college, and the middle sister was a freshman t a top engineering school. Their mother reported hat Anne had been an active toddler, difficult to ontrol. Her speech milestones (first word, first sentence, development of fluency) had been slightly late. As a young child, almost any change in the *status quo* ould set off temper tantrums. From kindergarten n, her teachers had said she was bright but not an chiever. She stared out the windows too much, fidgeted t her desk, did not complete her homework on time. Since the third grade, she had had minor behavioral problems in class. She was aggressive toward the eachers and was often sent to the principal's office.

The other girls her age disliked her for being "pushy," and she was socially isolated. When her parents made demands, she would become defiant. By the seventh and eighth grade, her mood swings became more intense and frequent. She skipped school frequently and became promiscuous. Many of these symptoms suggested the classic ADHD package, but often this goes undiagnosed in girls, probably because these girls are still less disruptive than many ADHD boys.

Anne's parents did bring her for psychiatric evaluation after she had run away from home for several days. She had gone to a big city with an older boy and stayed while their money lasted. A thorough physical exam and laboratory testing found nothing abnormal. An IQ test placed her in the bright-normal range, but other testing showed that she was readily distracted and did not easily direct her attention where others pointed. Her antisocial behavior was still less violent than we often see in teenage boys but this is typical of the self-destructive quality in many girls' antisocial behavior. Her promiscuity and growing drinking horrified her parents, but hurt her more than society.

We concluded that Anne probably had a long-standing attention-deficit hyperactivity disorder, which during the past two years had been leading to greater impulsivity and mood swings. A therapeutic trial of the stimulant Ritalin appeared successful. Anne began receiving As and Bs in school, and for the first time, started talking about an interest in going to college. She could complete chores at home and began making friends at school. Anne's treatment included psychological therapy to help improve her self-esteem and resolve the feelings of inadequacy that came from being the one child in a high-achieving family who had chronic academic difficulties.

CONDUCT DISORDER OR
SEIZURE DISORDER?

When Thomas first came to us he previously had been hospitalized twice in other institutions. The first hospital had diagnosed a conduct disorder complicated by drug and alcohol abuse. Later that diagnosis was changed to schizophrenia. His mother wanted a second opinion about this new diagnosis. She reported that Thomas had been an active toddler who had sustained several head injuries. When he was three an ear infection led to meningitis. His early school years had been marked by inattention and defiance of his teachers.

When he was fourteen Thomas joined a gang, stole a car while drunk and, on a dare, drove it straight into a tree. He sustained a head injury and a mild concussion. Two months later, he began expressing paranoid thoughts; he had visual and auditory hallucinations as well. After three days of growing confusion and agitation he said he feared he would be poisoned and he tried to jump from the roof of the family garage. He was hospitalized in an acutely psychotic state and was in a stupor for a week. A therapeutic trial of lithium brought moderate improvement and he was sent home.

Within three weeks he appeared less withdrawn, but he began to sleep only three hours each night and wandered around the house. He stole his mother's checkbook and forged checks to buy records. He used hallucinogenic drugs (PCP and LSD) and drank great amounts of alcohol. He was returned to a psychiatric hospital when he began expressing delusions of grandeur. He did not respond to antipsychotic medication and was given electroshock therapy after he tried to jump from a hospital window. It was shortly after that incident that Thomas's mother came to us.

The medical history revealed a complicated picture. Thomas had sustained head injuries and had an abnormal EEG. We reported to his parents that he appeared to have temporal lobe syndrome, an epilepsy like condition. The diagnosis surprised the mother who said she had "never seen him have a seizure." We explained that in our clinical work we saw many teenagers who had never had a seizure but who did have "epilepsy-related mood disorders" as described by Dr. J. Himmelhoch. Usually these kids had been diagnosed as being bipolar (shifting between elation and depression) or atypically depressed. These adolescents would often have an abnormal EEG or history of high fevers and convulsions as a child, or minor head injuries during middle childhood. Sometimes there would be a history of meningitis or even encephalitis.

Although Thomas's history provided a classic example of a child at risk for such a seizure disorder, his mother was still uncertain. She wondered why it had taken so long for the effects to appear. We responded that the explanation might lie in the recent theory of "kindling" as expounded by Drs. Ballenger, Post, and Kopanda. This theory proposes that the past injuries to the brain may not leave evident damage, but do put the brain at risk for further disorder. Kindling suggests that the injury can create new focal points in the brain where a seizure might begin if the neurons at that point become sufficiently excited. And once having been "kindled," these focal points may become sites for further seizures. Later experiences in life that might do no long-term harm to an ordinary person can have a devastating effect on an at-risk individual. In Thomas's case, we suspected that his use of cocaine "kindled" the seizures. Drugs of abuse, particularly cocaine, cause great changes in the functioning of even a healthy brain, and they can have devastating effects on anyone who is at risk for this kindling phenomenon.

We prescribed Tegretol (carbamazepine), an anticonvulsant, "antikindling" medication often used in the treatment of seizure disorders. The drug reduced his irritability and mood instability. Nine months later, the visual and auditory hallucinations had completely ceased, along with his delusions of grandeur, paranoia, and violent behavior. He entered residential treatment for two years, living in a special school that worked on his educational problems and drug use. Today Thomas has graduated from high school. He has a part-time job, is an active participant in AA-NA, and is planning to enter junior college.

CONDUCT DISORDER OR BIPOLAR DISORDER?

Thirteen-year-old Jennifer was referred to us by a psychologist who had given her individual therapy for one year. She had entered therapy when she developed sleep problems, a decline in school grades, and temper tantrums at home and with her friends. Her therapist reported that her self-esteem was poor, she reacted badly to change, and responded poorly to any perceived pressures at home or school. Severe anxiety often kept her awake, especially on school nights. Her teachers said she had trouble reading at grade level.

During the six months before our evaluation (but after the original therapy had begun), Jennifer began to lie frequently to her mother about schoolwork, and she often cut class. Her "yelling and screaming fits," as her mother called them, were growing worse. At home she often responded in rage to requests that she make minor decisions, such as what movie to see. Often these rages lasted ten to twenty minutes. In a typical episode she would throw herself on the floor, threaten suicide, push her mother, and cry profusely; just as abruptly Jennifer would become quiet and apologize to her family for her behavior.

Her behavior was growing more aggressive and

destructive. She often broke property during her rages.
Her mother had recently discovered a bag of mari-
juana in Jennifer's drawer and worried about the
extent of her daughter's drug use. Her father reported
that there had been several episodes in which she
became giggly, silly, and spoke fast. He also reported
that she had taken $200 received for her birthday
and spent it all at once on clothing.

A physical examination, laboratory testing, and
EEG showed Jennifer's medical condition, including
that of her central nervous system, to be normal.
There was no history of head injury or significant
medical problems. The family's psychiatric history,
however, revealed a maternal grandmother and a
maternal aunt who had both suffered "nervous break-
downs." Her aunt's condition had been treated, with
partial success, with lithium, while her grandmother
had received a course of electroconvulsive therapy
(ECT). In addition, Jennifer's father was a recovering
alcoholic.

A search for a successful treatment took some
time. We initially treated Jennifer with a tricyclic
antidepressant, for her condition appeared to be an
agitated depression. Her mother reported that Jennifer's tantrums grew more violent and more frequent,
and that her mood swings became more severe. Because of her family's psychiatric history of probable
bipolar disorder, in which patients move rapidly from
the two "polar" extremes of elation and depression,
we decided to stop the antidepressant, hypothesizing
that it had caused "pharmacological hypomania."

We shifted her to a lithium treatment. Her depressive symptoms did decrease, but the tantrums
and irritability continued. Adding Tegretol to her
medication regimen gradually reduced the frequency
and intensity of these outbursts. Jennifer's antisocial
patterns ended, and her defiant behavior eased. Her
schoolwork improved. She continued in individual
therapy to treat her poor self-esteem and her difficulty making friends. Her psychologist reports that she

has now shown considerable progress in these areas, too.

CONDUCT DISORDER OR DEPRESSION?

When he was fifteen, Danny was found guilty of breaking-and-entering charges. The court sent him to us for psychiatric evaluation. His parents reported that about a year before this consultation, Danny had seemed unhappy and was losing interest in his friends. Previously he had been an obedient child, but now he ignored household rules and neglected his chores. At times he grew antagonistic and irritable, but then would swing "almost back to normal." During his gloomy period his parents had been especially worried by the suicide of one of Danny's close friends. It came after the boy had fought with his parents about his poor grades. Danny said he "envied" his friend because "his problems are ended." Eventually his spirits did begin to lift, but at the same time Danny began stealing large sums of money from his mother, tried to withdraw money from a cash machine using his father's bank card, and broke into a neighbor's house, stealing and pawning antique silver. After the robbery Danny was arrested and taken to a youth shelter where he tried to hang himself with his belt. A judge sentenced him to three years' probation, at which time he was referred to us.

During the year before coming to us Danny had been referred to a psychologist who recommended intensive individual therapy for depression. After a few months, Danny refused to speak during these sessions. The psychologist reluctantly ended the therapy when Danny's parents complained. They next tried family therapy which again ended abruptly after Danny refused to attend. Although Danny showed strong signs of depression his parents thought he seemed "more angry than depressed." Like many people, they assumed that depression means feeling sad and reclusive; often, however, the symptoms of depression are anger and increased agitation.

Danny's first therapist assured his parents that he was "in a state of adolescent turmoil" rather than clinically depressed. He advised against referral to a psychiatrist, saying he did not believe in the use of medication for teenagers because it would lead them to believe that "a pill could solve all their problems."

The second therapist said that once Danny's hostile relationship with his parents improved the depression would disappear. His pediatrician, who had initially tried to counsel Danny, became angry when Danny stole some free samples of an antihistamine from his desk. Danny said that in the past he had felt calmer after taking an allergy pill and that he was attempting to medicate his own symptoms.

We conducted a physical examination, family history, laboratory testing, and an EEG. All the results were normal, with one important exception. Danny had undergone a dexamethasome suppression test, which checks for a possible biological basis for clinical depression. Danny's results were extremely high. This test, combined with Danny's recent history, indicated major depression. We prescribed nortriptyline, a tricyclic antidepressant, and after two weeks his mood disorder appeared to wane. His parents reported decreased irritability and anger, improved schoolwork, and renewed interest in friends. He began to do his household chores and to mend his relationship with his brother and sisters. No further evidence of conduct disorder appeared. A year later Danny was on the school honor roll and a busy participant in local activities.

PREVENTION TECHNIQUES

The obvious first step in preventing the development of conduct disorder is to treat whatever has put a child at risk. ADHD, for example, may put the child at risk for a conduct disorder; controlling the ADHD is an important step in preventing the rise of antisocial complications.

Also, psychologists have worked to develop programs that can prevent conduct disorders by teaching children to think in socially successful ways. The most promising results have been obtained by programs that teach specific ways of solving problems. More general programs based on traditional ideas, such as the belief that getting a job teaches responsibility, or that becoming active in a community promotes social caring, have been, at best, disappointments.

An especially successful prevention system is the Primary Mental Health Project developed in Rochester, New York. It began almost thirty years ago and is now found in schools scattered across the land. The project identifies at-risk children in kindergarten through the third grade, and for half a year puts them in a once-a-week session that lasts about three quarters of an hour. Sometimes the children attend a small class; more often a child receives individual attention. Before they get down to the details of their lessons, teachers work to establish close relationships with each child. Then they teach the children how to understand the feelings of others and how to think about new ways to behave. Children also learn how to set limits on their own behavior and about the difference between feeling angry and acting angry. This latter point is subtle and important. Children need to know that it is natural and okay to feel angry, but acting on the feeling is another matter.

The Rochester approach is much admired, and many other school systems have either adopted it outright or developed their own variation. One variation introduces training into preschool. It provides immediate help to children who have trouble adjusting to school routine. The preschoolers are taught ways to think about getting along with friends and with schoolwork. Parents also come for lessons in how to help their children develop good social behavior. Followup studies indicate that the participants do get enduring benefits from the program.

But, valuable as they are, these teaching programs can only be a second line of preventive defense. They do help children, but they help some more than others, and disruptive aggressive children get the least benefit. The primary difficulty of disruptively disordered children is that they do not control, and sometimes cannot control their actions. Teaching them better ways of acting is a good idea, but it works best only when the primary problems are treated. The key to preventing the development of a conduct disorder lies in helping the children get control over their own behavior and in teaching families how to help their child become more responsible and social. If children get good primary help, a program such as Rochester's Primary Mental Health Project holds much promise.

SUICIDE

In some cases, conduct-disordered children may become murderously violent. Their most common victim is themselves. Suicide is a growing problem among American teenagers, and conduct-disordered children are particularly at risk. This finding will surprise some readers, for we are used to thinking of antisocial people, young or old, as being egotists. Killing oneself is the ultimate assault on one's own ego and thus sounds out of character; however, the character of conduct-disordered children is complex. Instead of thinking highly of themselves, CD children may actually suffer from low self-esteem. They are also impulsive and aggressive, and can suddenly turn that aggression on themselves.

There are about 500,000 suicide attempts by teenagers each year, and more than 5,000 actual suicides. That works out to more than 1,000 attempts and over twelve suicides per day! Self-murder is the second leading cause of death among fifteen-to-twenty-four-year-olds. Adolescents who combine symptoms of conduct disorder and depression are at high risk for suicide. The strong association of depression and suicide, of course, is well established, but depression is not the only psychiatric condition associated with suicide.

One recent study of over 100 preteenagers who showed either suicidal or assaultive tendencies found that almost half of them combined depression with aggression. A further study of thirty teenagers who had successfully committed suicide, found that over half of them were both antisocial and depressed. Other research has found an important distinction between thinking about suicide and really trying it. Depressed children think about it more than antisocial youths, but the antisocial group is more likely to try, and, if they attempt, are more likely to succeed. A person who is depressed, aggressive, and so impulsive that he constantly acts against his own self-interest is seriously at risk for suicide. If we add ready access to guns and drugs to the picture, it becomes even more dangerous. One large study of jailed juvenile delinquents found that 70 percent of them had shown suicidal tendencies during the year before their incarceration. Sixty percent of them had made at least one suicide attempt.

Suicide prevention parallels the techniques for preventing the development of conduct disorder. The first step is accurately spotting the at-risk child. It is particularly important to discover the depression. Teenage depression is very treatable, and help will greatly reduce the danger of a suicide attempt. The family should also be helped. Suicidal children often come from homes where the parents are depressed. Alcohol problems and unstable family relationships may be common. The size of the risks are ominous, but by taking them seriously and acting to avert them, they can be conquered.

EVALUATING A CONDUCT DISORDER

Many psychiatric disorders make life miserable for the patients who endure them, and conduct-disordered children are no exception. Any account that dwells on their state of mind can quickly create sympathy for them, but conduct-disordered children also produce a long list of victims—the innocent targets of their actions. These unfortunates may have been beaten, robbed, burned out of their homes, or even murdered. Naturally, the victims, with whom ordinary citizens can readily identify, get more sympathy than the perpetrators. In most cases, a psychiatric diagnosis raises the question of what can be done to help the patient. A diagnosis of conduct disorder, however, often provokes a response of what can be done to protect society from the patient. This loaded reaction makes the diagnosis more than routinely difficult to reach. A doctor who is wrong has marked a child with an indelible pen. Suspected conduct disorder is among the most common reasons schools and juvenile courts refer a child for psychiatric evaluation. Clearly, labeling a youngster as conduct-disordered can have many ramifications.

Treating conduct-disordered children is also difficult and uncertain. There are no sure ways to control antisocial behavior in a conduct-disordered child, so a misdiagnosis may keep someone from getting the treatment he needs. A doctor who makes an alternate diagnosis, however, can point to a possible treatment. Our work has shown that treatment can be very effective when another diagnosis is present.

Suspected conduct disorder is *always* accompanied by symptoms and features that point an examiner in several possible directions. The most visible accompanying symptoms are an attention-deficit and hyperactivity. Indeed, ADHD is so commonly a part of an antisocial child's history that the relationship between conduct disorder and ADHD has been extensively studied. A child with an attention deficit does not necessarily become conduct-disordered, but a conduct-disordered child frequently has an attention deficit. Sometimes treating the ADHD can resolve the antisocial behavior in someone who had seemed hopelessly conduct-disordered.

Antisocial children also do poorly in school. During the evaluation of a child referred because of antisocial behavior, we routinely hear about a child who has poor marks, has repeated a school grade or two, and has endless problems with homework. The search for root causes is an important part of the evaluation. Is a child doing poorly in school because he is conduct-disordered, or does the antisocial behavior arise from the frustrations of doing poorly in school? An antisocial child with a learning disability may improve his behavior if the disability is treated.

Antisocial children tend to have few or no friends. If they do have peers to whom they are loyal, the peers tend to be antisocial as well. They may form gangs because of their members' attraction to violence, vandalism, or drugs. Other children reject both the loner and the antisocial gangs because of their disruptiveness, cruelty, and unfairness. Again, there is no automatic way to distinguish cause from effect. Has a child's antisocial behavior produced peer rejection, or has peer rejection produced antisocial behavior?

By itself, an antisocial action is not always abnormal or even unusual. Fighting, stealing, and lying are a common part of many childhoods, so some parents are slow to take alarm when their child misbehaves. They expect the child to outgrow it in the normal process of socialization. The reasonableness of this assumption can be seen by comparing two playgrounds. Watch the play area of a grade school.

Most of the children are running about having a fine time, but scuffles and fights break out fairly often. Now watch the playing field of a high school. Uproars are not unknown, but they are less common. In the normal course of growth, there is a decline in antisocial actions. Lies are much more frequent among seven-year-olds than among twelve-year-olds. Aggressive behavior declines as well. Of course, individual differences persist as the children age.

Conduct-disordered children show a markedly different pattern. They grow wilder as they get older. As other children get over their tendency to throw tantrums, these children persist and their tantrums may even grow louder and more violent. They continue to fight, steal, skip school, destroy property, threaten others, and run away from home. Few children are so severely disordered as to do all these things, but a conduct-disordered child continues some of them. In particular, their antisocial behavior is frequent and can have unusually severe consequences. The greater the consequences, the less frequent an action has to be for it to be a warning sign. Skipping class once probably does not mean much, but routine truancy is a warning sign. For inherently serious actions, like setting fire to a building, just one such action is a warning of trouble and must be investigated.

Because of the frequency and severity of their antisocial behavior, conduct-disordered children often have contact with many social services. School disciplinarians, social workers, and court officers commonly know about their cases before any psychiatrist is called in for an evaluation. These people may have labeled the child as a "delinquent." Juvenile delinquents and conduct-disordered children are sometimes the same people, but not always. Delinquency is an administrative term used by various social and legal services. It can apply to a youth who has gotten into bad trouble, but who had previously functioned acceptably. A conduct-disordered person's impairment is such that it can affect every aspect of his daily life.

ALTERNATE DIAGNOSES

Juvenile delinquency has been a focus of social concern for decades. Much of the discussion has asked whom to blame. One group says the kids are "rotten" and should be treated like any other criminals. Another group blames society for failing to provide a more secure socioeconomic environment for the children. The first group retorts, "Oh, yeah, then how come most of the children who grow up in poor conditions do not become delinquents?" To which the reformers say, "Then explain why it is always the poor neighborhoods that produce so much of the delinquency." This debate has been going around in circles for generations without really hitting on anything fundamentally new.

A possible third explanation is that the children suffer from a medical disorder that leads to poverty and social disarray. A child with untreated conduct disorder often grows into a troubled adult—one that may have difficulty finding or holding a job, suffer from drug abuse or addiction, or turn to crime. Their offspring may inherit poverty and social disarray along with a medical condition that leads to conduct disorder.

Over the past decade, evidence has grown that children who could be diagnosed as having conduct disorders have other problems as well. Antisocial children frequently grow up to be psychotic or suffer from other psychiatric conditions. Were they that way as youths but the examiners were too impatient or frightened to notice? A prominent psychiatrist, Dr. Dorothy O. Lewis, has studied the early lives of antisocial children, and has found that they have extremely complex medical and neurological histories. They suffer more accidents and injuries, and they spend more time in hospitals than normal children usually do. Symptoms of epilepsy are unusually common in very violent children.

Furthermore, her studies of the psychiatric symptoms of violent delinquents have demonstrated that 38 percent reported visual hallucinations, 43 percent reported hearing voices, 60 percent showed confused thinking, and 82 percent had paranoid symptoms. Over half of them had been hospitalized previously for psychiatric reasons. When evaluating an antisocial child an examiner should ask about previous episodes of poor motor control and temper outbursts, drinking and drug use, a history of psychosis, attention deficit, epilepsy, and/or head injury, family history of seizures or other neurological problems.

A classic description of disruptively disordered children is contained in Michael Rutter's report on children growing up on the Isle of Wight, an island just off the southern coast of Britain. Rutter's data showed that serious reading difficulties and antisocial behavior often go together. Evaluating an antisocial child is not a search for an easy label. It looks at a host of risks and tries to make sense of them as they apply to a particular unhappy child.

CHAPTER 9

Treating
Conduct Disorders

Our work with seriously antisocial children does not point toward a single "best" treatment. As with any disruptive disorder, it is the reaction of other people to the behavior that usually sends a person to a clinic. If a youth is particularly violent, destructive, or threatening, society understandably wants to find some direct way of stopping or controlling that behavior. We have seen, however, that antisocial children have varied reasons for behaving as they do, and many of these reasons have nothing directly to do with their environmental circumstances.

Studies indicate that differences in socioeconomic status per se do not cause antisocial behavior. However, it is the differences in various social conditions (such as poor housing, limited resources, poor medical care, and increased stress) that account for the increase in antisocial behavior in the lower socioeconomic groups. Socioeconomic stresses surely make it much easier for a disordered child to fall through the cracks and receive no help until he becomes a serious social threat. A child who may benefit from ADHD treatment at age seven but is ignored will no longer be ignored when, at age thirteen, his disruptions become dangerously antisocial. Yet even at that late date, the root cause of the problem remains the attention deficit and it needs to be treated. The many social and educational problems that have wrapped themselves around the core problem need to be addressed as well, but they cannot be resolved until we take control of any physical cause of the disorder.

We believe that many cases of antisocial behavior should be treated just as we would treat any other medical problem. Step 1 is to examine the patient and attempt to make a precise diagnosis. Step 2 is to treat the patient in accordance with the diagnosis. Sometimes there will be Steps 3 and 4, which concern complicating factors and long-term health. A child who has been bitten by rats, for example, should be treated for bites *and* the rats at home should be exterminated. To fight the rats and ignore the bite would be absurd. To treat the bite and ignore the rats would be equally absurd. Conduct-disordered patients need similarly thorough care.

MEDICATIONS

Often, part of our treatment involves medication. People sometimes say that disruptive children with ADHD can be helped by medications, but not disruptive children with antisocial disorders. Our experience suggests otherwise. Medication frequently is the key to taking initial control of a disorder. When psychiatry first began using drugs to treat conduct disorder the basic idea was to calm the patients enough so that behavior modification therapy could have some hope of taking effect. More recently, however, the attitude has begun to change as a diagnosis of conduct disorder has been found to be accompanied by other, more treatable conditions such as depression, or seizure, bipolar, and attention-deficit hyperactivity disorders. Behavior modification and family or individual therapies contribute too, but, as we saw in the case histories described in the previous chapter, the medication is important.

Tricyclic Antidepressants (TCAs)

Two of the case studies cited in the previous chapter included medication with a TCA. Jennifer, who was successfully treated for bipolar disorder, was first treated with a TCA. At that time we suspected unipolar depressive disorder and TCAs can help in such cases. Her poor response led us to reconsider and treat the disorder with mood stabilizers, lithium and Tegretol. We had greater success with TCAs with Danny, the boy whose close friend had committed suicide. A prescription of the TCA nortriptyline led to a marked reduction in his depression. His case showed how effective medication can be in treating children who are at risk for suicide.

TCAs are a promising treatment for antisocial youths whose behavior meets the psychiatric criteria for depression. Their use, however, must be closely monitored. An overdose can be fatal, so the pills should be kept in a safe place, out of the reach of the patient. Teenagers may object to being "treated like a child," but a depressed adolescent may have an overwhelming impulse to take an overdose of TCA. Used properly, however, the medication can be most effective.

As noted in Chapter 7, TCAs are sometimes used instead of stimulants when treating ADHD. Two especially common drugs used in ADHD cases are desipramine and imipramine. Desipramine often has milder side effects. Response to TCAs, if there is one, is usually much quicker in ADHD than in depression; however, for some ADHD children, the drug may lose its effectiveness over time.

Lithium

A reliable and indispensable medication for the treatment of mania, lithium has been increasingly used in treating antisocial children, since it helps reduce aggression. Lithium has been shown to help in cases of conduct-disordered children who are given to aggressive and explosive outbursts. Children whose parents respond well to lithium appear to respond especially well to lithium treatment. Sometimes in the treatment of depression, we will combine a TCA with lithium, in order to increase the effectiveness of the TCA. Lithium requires careful monitoring, including laboratory tests and an EKG.

Carbamazepine (Tegretol)

The drug of choice in controlling temporal-lobe epilepsy, Tegretol, is becoming increasingly common in other treatments as well. It has been found to succeed in the treatment of bipolar patients with whom lithium proved ineffective, or partially effective. A Tegretol trial is plausible in many serious childhood disorders in which the ordinary "first-line" treatments do not succeed. This option is possible because side effects have proven less dangerous than once feared. Concern about possible blood-cell abnormalities once limited its use, but further research has shown that Tegretol is a fairly safe medication when prescribed properly and carefully monitored. Our experience has been that Tegretol can be effective in many adolescent disorders involving aggressive behavior, mood swings, and explosive outbursts.

Valproic acid (Depakote) and clonazepam (Klonopin) are also anticonvulsants which may have a role in treating these disorders.

Propranolol

Explosive rages in adults can often be controlled by this medication. Its use with children and teenagers is less common, but has been successful in several cases, especially where there may be neurological factors contributing to the youngster's problem. Potential side effects include dizziness, sedation, a slow heart rate, depression, and an upset stomach.

BEHAVIORAL MODIFICATION

Treatments that involve training or counseling are most promising when, like the best medication, they are aimed at specific problems. Three areas in particular that often require attention are damage within a family, the absence of social skills, and educational problems.

Every family suffers when it includes a severely antisocial child. Commonly, parents and children develop ways of interacting that make the problems and irritations worse. These behaviors are probably not the cause of a conduct disorder, but they can exacerbate it and make recovery more difficult. Even after medication has overcome the basic problem, people do not automatically change old patterns of interacting. Parents of antisocial children often develop practices that promote aggressive behavior. Parents may, without realizing it, reward the conduct they are trying to stop. In a busy home, for example, a child may discover that the one sure way to gain attention is by misbehaving badly. Suddenly a busy household makes him the center of interest and concern. The effect can be to strengthen a tendency to act up. Some important therapies include:

Parent Management Training

In this approach the therapist works with the parents and does not directly treat the child. It is the parents who learn how to be on-site therapists. They learn ways to strengthen desirable behavior by praising and rewarding a child for proper conduct. They also learn effective ways of punishing a child without turning the incident into something so great it becomes its own reward. Although the training can yield a marked improvement, it makes real demands on the parents. They must be willing to attend training sessions, to practice what they learn, and to use the program at home. Some parents are too busy, exhausted, or uninterested to make the necessary effort.

Functional Family Therapy

The goal of this approach is similar to parent management training. It too aims to increase rewards and make punishment more effective. Instead of focusing so much on techniques, however, it tries to get families to think about what they are trying to do in a particular situation. By finding new ways to think about old problems, they can seek out better ways of interacting.

Cognitive Problem-Solving Skills Therapy

During infancy all children are impulsive. As they grow older they learn how to see things in perspective. But disruptive children do not outgrow their impulsivity so quickly, and children who become conduct-disordered may not outgrow it at all. Even if medication does help overcome the problem, the children are still years behind their peers in learning such basics of survival as hunting for better alternatives, or thinking of what series of actions has to come between a desire and its satisfaction. They need practice at imagining the consequences of their action and at grasping how one event causes another. They especially need to understand how their actions affect their relations with others. Problem-solving therapy teaches children how to put things in perspective. The therapist works with the child, usually taking an active role in teaching these skills.

Conduct disorder is a frightening prospect and an even more disturbing reality. The best treatment is prevention by identifying the source of risk and treating that. Barring that solution, a careful, precise diagnosis and assessment can lead to a successful treatment plan. Then medication and therapy can combine to help make the future bright.

PART IV

After They
Are Grown

CHAPTER 10

The Outcome

Every parent must at some time worry, What is going to become of my child? The question presses with even greater force if a child seems unable to adapt to the demands of childhood. What can the future hold for boys and girls who cannot even master second grade? To us adults, being a grown-up seems harder and more demanding. But for disruptively disordered children, second grade may be life's greatest challenge. School tests their handicap head-on, and learning how to cope with it suggests they are capable of facing the roughest things life can present.

Rumor, hope, and fear long dominated any discussion about the destiny of children diagnosed as having a disruptive disorder. At first, ADHD was thought to be something that children simply outgrew; in part this belief arose because some children do eventually put the disorder behind them. Many a restless and fidgety seven-year-old seems normal at

117

eighteen. This hopeful prediction that the problem
will simply fade away like last winter's snow comforted
many parents, but eventually there came a rude
awakening.

Disruptive disorders are not symptoms of prolonged toddlerhood, or emotional repression. They
arise from biological problems, which may recede in
time but often continue. Some symptoms do change,
however; the uncontrollable second-grader who is
dragged screaming from a classroom by an over-
wrought teacher may not experience anything like
that in tenth grade. But the problems of inattention,
impulsivity, and overactivity may persist and pro-
voke new difficulties. The fact that the disruptive
problems can persist well beyond puberty at times
leads parents to be fearful that their disruptive child
might be doomed to become antisocial, to experience
job failure, and to suffer personal misery. The future
does not appear to be so bleak.

Do disruptive children become antisocial as they
grow up? We have seen in Part III that there is some
risk of such a development, but we must be careful
not to overstate it. We have also seen many cases
where the risk was deflected and remained so. Followup studies on ADHD youngsters who were diagnosed in childhood have found that approximately 25
percent of the adolescents have conduct disorders.
ADHD adolescents appear to have lower academic
achievement and suffer from low self-esteem. A defin-
itive future for these children is unclear, but the good
news is that the majority of hyperactive youngsters
do not turn out to be antisocial adults. Commenting
on their own fifteen-year followup study of hyperactive youngsters, as well as on other related studies in
their book *Hyperactive Children Grown Up*, Doctors
Gabriella Weiss and Lily T. Hechtman state that
"the concern may be exaggerated and that few hyperactive children grow up to be serious adult offenders."

One study found that the young adult who had
not outgrown the three main features of ADHD—

inattention, impulsivity, and overactivity—is at much greater risk for having significant antisocial behavior.

We still need to learn more about the everyday lives of former ADHD children who have become adults. In fact, the presence of ADHD in adults is an area that has just recently been recognized. How prevalent the disorder is is unclear, but it has been estimated that it could be as high as five percent. The few studies done indicate stimulants may also be effective for this older age group.

One subject of concern is the effect of spending years on medication. Taking stimulants for a few times a day for years is not to be recommended lightly. Although children may report some side effects when the drug is introduced, most report tolerating the medication well over time. There have been conflicting reports over the long-term effect of stimulants on height and weight development. Therefore, we urge that children receiving stimulants have their height and weight levels monitored by a physician at regular intervals.

The question has been asked regarding whether years of taking medication create drug and/or alcohol abusers. At present, there is no evidence to support this view. In addition, the majority of ADHD children, whether treated or not, do not end up as drug abusers. Therefore childhood ADHD by itself does not appear to lead to substance abuse disorders. One study found that in late adolescence and early adulthood, when ADHD was accompanied by conduct disorder, then there was a greater incidence of drug abuse. The substance abuse generally began at the same time or following the onset of the conduct disorder. Therefore the link may be strongest between conduct disorder and substance abuse, as opposed to between ADHD and substance abuse.

MAKING IT

ADHD adults fit roughly into three categories. One group has outgrown or overcome the problem. The impulsivity, inattention, and restlessness have gone or are much better controlled, just as everybody had hoped. These people comprise approximately 30 to 40 percent of the whole.

The largest group, approximately 40 to 50 percent, continues to have symptoms of impulsive behavior and/or restlessness and/or inattention. Despite significant difficulties, these people do not have severe psychiatric problems or antisocial behavior. Even without fully outgrowing the problem, they are able to lead self-sufficient lives.

The third group is comprised of a minority of about one in ten who are severely dysfunctional. As adults they may require hospitalization, or even end up in jail. We believe this minority could be made even smaller if treatment and help were more readily available and were followed more rigorously.

One study found that when asked what helped them most during childhood, ADHD young adults most often indicated the presence of a parent who never doubted their final success, or a teacher who took the trouble to care.

Success in anyone's life means finding one's niche, the place where one can excel and be happy. Many adults who were disruptive children report that important progress came with the discovery of some special talent they had that gave them the confidence to claim a place in the world.

Among celebrities, we have found none whose biography lists a childhood disruptive disorder, but if you listen to some of them tell how they entered the profession that made them famous, you can hear some familiar-sounding memories. Comedians, especially, tend to tell a recognizable story. Their stock tale says that as children they were not particularly

ppy. School bored them; the other children disliked
em; but then they discovered a special key to
opularity. They could make their classmates laugh,
they developed that skill.

Although only a minority of any group can be-
me successful performers, each of us can fit in
mewhere. In a performer's childhood memories we
e that handicaps often point toward their own
lution. It still takes talent and effort to follow that
ide, but childhood—even a difficult one—is a time
r discovering one's own tastes and talents. It is
portant not to discourage or scorn a child's ability,
en if the skill is used inappropriately. Encourage a
ild to develop a talent in its proper context.

The first crisis in the life of many disruptive
ildren comes when they enter school and realize
at school is not their niche. Fortunately, as they
ow older, they will have a wider variety of places to
plore. Each child must find his own place, but
rtain characteristics make the most promising niches.

ommon Sense Over Book Sense

Although there may have been some brilliant
holars who began life with ADHD, school is often
ot the ADHD child's area of greatest achievement.
ne study of ADHD children found that in early
dulthood (a mean age of 21 years old), only 20
ercent were in school. In a matched group of non-
DHD children, slightly over half (53 percent) were
ontinuing full-time education. College and further
ducation are certainly not impossible for ADHD
ildren; however, they may find they are more suc-
ssful in non-academic areas.

ocial Over Impersonal Interactions

When asked what they found most satisfying
out their work, former ADHD children often say
ey appreciate the social contact it gives them.
ther people are more likely to focus on the chal-
nge and learning opportunity their work provides,

but an appreciation of abstractions may not accompany ADHD.

Active Over Sedentary Labor

Adults who were hyperactive children often choose more active jobs. This finding can hardly be surprising. It may mean simply that as adults these people know who they are and how to satisfy their tastes. An active job does not necessarily mean someone who is on the go all the time, like a hotel bellhop or a shortstop. It can mean someone who moves about, goes to different meetings, sees different people, or operates different pieces of equipment. As adults these people are not as active and rambunctious as they were when they were eight, but they may still need more activity than other people their age.

Broadly speaking, these categories outline the sort of work settings where ADHD grown-ups may do best. It may take a little longer for these ADHD people to find their niche. Some studies suggest that when they first finish school ADHD young adults change jobs more often than other graduates. But in general, hyperactive adults are able to be self-sufficient and fully employed.

Self-esteem continues to be a problem for the young adult hyperactive. However, early intervention may help to prevent this negative self-esteem. Interestingly, a study comparing young adults who had been treated in childhood for ADHD with stimulant medications to young adults with a history of ADHD without stimulant treatment found that the stimulant-treated group had better social skills and a more positive self-regard. In addition, the stimulant-treated group reported a lower incidence of car accidents, a more positive view of childhood, fewer problems with aggression, and reduced need for psychiatric care when compared to the non-stimulant-treated group.

What do researchers tell us about the outcome of the anti-social child, the child with a conduct disor-

er? We know that aggressiveness does not diminish
ver time. In *Deviant Children Grown Up*, Dr. L. N.
Robins describes a group of antisocial children stud-
ed over a period of 30 years. As they grew into
dolescence and adulthood, these children showed
onsiderably more psychiatric symptoms, engaged in
more criminal activity and showed poorer social
unctioning in general than a control group. We know
hat only approximately 50 percent of a group of
onduct-disordered children will develop into antiso-
ial adults. But this is not the full story. Of the group
f conduct-disordered children who do not develop
nto antisocial adults, a high percentage will have
ther psychiatric disabilities including drug and al-
ohol abuse. These adults are likely to have more
sychiatric hospitalizations, to be unemployed or
nderemployed, to drop out of school or achieve less
n school. They are more likely to have impaired
narital and family relationships with more frequent
livorces and remarriages. They will tend to be less
ctive in community affairs and to have higher arrest
ates for drunken driving and criminal acts.

Two factors point to an ominous prognosis: The
arlier in a child's life history the antisocial behav-
ors emerge, and the greater the frequency of these
ehaviors. Antisocial children with antisocial or sub-
tance abusing parents are at particularly high risk
or becoming antisocial adults. The child with a long
listory of multiple antisocial behaviors at home, in
he community, and at school, is at particularly high
isk, especially if these behaviors include aggressiveness
oward others. The family with major problems—poor
upervision of the child, child abuse, marital conflict,
parental substance abuse—provides the breeding
ground for the antisocial adult.

Dr. Alan E. Kazdin proposes a "chronic disease
model" for conduct disorder which is very helpful in
our understanding of the natural course and treatment of this disorder. He observes in his book, *Conduct Disorder in Childhood and Adolescence:*

one medical model ... may prompt an important approach for the treatment of conduct disorder, namely that of chronic disease. Among many diseases, diabetes mellitus is relatively familiar and one that illustrates the issues that are applicable to conduct disorder ... Diabetes is viewed as a chronic condition that is not treated in such a fashion that it will go away. Treatment is based on the assumption that the person suffers from a condition that requires continued care, management and treatment ... Research on conduct disorders suggests that it is very much like a chronic condition in terms of the development and course. Also, the dysfunction has broad impact during childhood (e.g., in affecting behavior at home and in school; interpersonal, academic, and cognitive spheres) and adulthood (e.g., psychological, social and work adjustment).

It is not accurate to think of a conduct disorder as an acute condition like a "strep throat" that can be "cured" by a course of antibiotics. The parents of the conduct-disordered child must expect multiple forms of treatment at each stage of the disorder, including behavioral and family therapy, and medication as needed. As in any chronic medical condition, there will be flare-ups and even emergencies which will require immediate intervention. As biopsychiatrists, we anticipate a good outcome for the conduct-disordered child who has had the benefit of such continuing treatment.

Sources

American Psychiatric Association, *Diagnostic and Statistical Manual of Mental Disorders*, Third Edition Revised. "Disorders Usually First Evident in Infancy, Childhood, or Adolescence," 1987.

Baroody, A.J. *Children's Mathematical Thinking: A Developmental Framework for Preschool, Primary, and Special Education Teachers*. New York: Columbia University Teachers College, 1987.

Biederman, J., et al. "Family-Genetic and Psychosocial Risk Factors in DSM-III Attention Deficit Disorder." *J Amer Acad Child Adolesc Psychiatry*, 29:526–533, 1990.

Blumer, D., Heilbronn, M., Himmelhock, J. "Indications for Carbamazepine in Mental Illness: Atypical Psychiatric Disorder or Temporal Lobe Syndrome?" *Comprehensive Psychiatry*, 29:108–122, 1988.

Bradley, C. "The Behavior of Children Receiving Benzedrine." *Am J of Psychiatry*, 94:577, 1937.

Bradley, C., Bowen, M. "Amphetamine (Benzedrine) Therapy of Children's Behavior Disorders." *Am J Orthopsychiatry*, 11:92–103, 1941.

Brent, D.A., et al. "Risk Factors for Adolescent Suicide: A Comparison of Adolescent Suicide Victims with Suicidal Inpatients." *Arch Gen Psychiatry*, 45: 581–588, 1988.

Brunstetter, R.W., Silver, L.B. "Attention Deficit Disorder." *Comprehensive Textbook of Psychiatry*, IV. Edited by Kaplan, H.I., and Sadock, B.J. Baltimore: William and Wilkins, 1985.

Campbell, M., Spencer, E.K. "Psychopharmacology in Child and Adolescent Psychiatry: A Review of the Past Five Years." *J Am Acad Child Adolesc Psychiatry*, 27(3):269–279, 1988.

Cantwell, D.P. "Psychiatric Illness in the Families of Hyperactive Children." *Arch Gen Psychiatry*, vol 27, Sept. 1972.

Carlson, G.A. "Bipolar Disorder in Adolescence." *Psychiatric Annals*, 15:379–386, 1985.

Chamberlain, P., Patterson, G.R. "Aggressive Behavior in Middle Childhood." *The Clinical Guide To Child Psychiatry*. Edited by Shaffer, D., et al. New York: The Free Press, 1985.

Conners, C.K., Wells, K.C. *Hyperkinetic Children: A Neuropsychosocial Approach*. Newbury Park, CA: Sage Publications, 1986.

Cotler, H.I. *Galaxy of Games, Stunts, and Activities for Elementary Physical Education*. West Nyack, NY: Parker Publishing, 1980.

Cowart, V.S. "The Ritalin Controversy: What's Made This Drug's Opponents Hyperactive?" *JAMA*, May 6, 1988.

Douglas, V.I. "Stop, Look and Listen: The Problem of Sustained Attention and Impulse Control in Hyperactive and Normal Children." *Com J Beh Science*, 4:259–282.

Dulcan, M.K. "The Psychopharmacologic Treatment of Children and Adolescents with Attention Deficit Disorder." *Psychiatric Annals*, 15:69, 1985.

Evans, R.W., Clay, T.H., Gualtieri, C.T. "Carbamazepine in Pediatric Psychiatry." *J Amer Acad Child Adolesc Psychiatry*, 26: 2–8, 1987.

Gittelman, R., et al. "Hyperactive Boys Almost Grown Up: I, Psychiatric Status." *Arch Gen Psychiatry*, 42:937–947, 1985.

Gittelman-Klein, R., et al. "Relative Efficacy of Methylphenidate and Behavior Modification in Hyperkinetic Children: An Interim Report." *J Abnormal Child Psychology*, 4:361–377, 1976.

Gittelman-Klein, R., et al. "Comparative Effects of Methylphenidate and Thioridazine in Hyperkinetic Children: Clinical Results." *Arch Gen Psychiatry*, 33:1217–1231, 1976.

Greenhill, L.L. "Attention Deficit Hyperactivity Disorder in Children." *Psychiatric Disorders in Children and Adolescents*. Edited by Garfinkel, B.D., et al. Philadelphia: W.B. Saunders, 1990.

Greenhill, L.L. "Pediatric Psychopharmacology" and "The Hyperkinetic Syndrome." *The Clinical Guide To Child Psychiatry* Edited by Shaffer, D., et al. New York: The Free Press, 1985.

Hunt, R.D., Sanders, R.Q. "Hyperactivity and Attention Deficit in Children and Adults: New Approaches." Paper for Vanderbilt University School of Medicine, August 1987.

Ingersoll, B. *Your Hyperactive Child: A Parent's Guide to Coping with Attention Deficit Disorder.* New York: Doubleday, 1988.

Jensen, P.S., Shervette, R.E., Xenakis, S.N., Blackwood,

A. "Anxiety and Depressive Disorders in ADD: New Findings and Alternative Models."

Kaufman, D.M. "Seizure." *Clinical Neurology for Psychiatrists*. New York: Grune and Stratton, 1986.

Kazdin, A.E. *Conduct Disorders in Childhood and Adolescence*, Newbury Park, CA: Sage Publications, 1987.

Kelso, J., Stewart, M.A. "Factors Which Predict the Persistence of Aggressive Conduct Disorder." *J Child Psych Psychoanal*, XXVII(1), 1986.

Kolata, G. "Consensus on Diets and Hyperactivity." *Science*, vol 215, Feb. 19, 1982.

Lewis, D.O. "Juvenile Delinquency." *The Clinical Guide to Child Psychiatry*. Edited by Shaffer, D., et al. New York: The Free Press, 1985.

Lewis, D.O., Balla, D.A. *Delinquency and Psychopathology*. New York: Grune and Stratton, 1976.

Lewis, D.O., et al. "Psychomotor Epilepsy and Violence in an Incarcerated Adolescent Population." *Am J Psychiatry*, 138: 882–887, 1981.

Lewis, D.O., et al. "Violent Juvenile Delinquents: Psychiatric, Neurological, Psychological and Abuse Factors." *J Am Acad Child Adolesc Psych*, 19:160–171, 1980.

Lou, H.C., Hendrickson, L., Bruhn, P. "Focal Cerebral Hypoperfusion in Children with Dysphasia and/or Attention-deficit Disorder." *Arch Neurol*, 41:825, 1984.

Mannuzza, S., et al. "Hyperactive Boys Almost Grown Up: II. Status of Subjects Without a Mental Disorder." *Arch Gen Psychiatry*, 45:13–18, 1988.

McKnew, D.H., et al. "Lithium in Children of Lithium-Responding Parents." *Psychiatry Research*, 4:171–180, 1981.

Morrison, J.R., Stewart, M.A. "The Psychiatric Status

of the Legal Families of Adopted Hyperactive Children." *Arch Gen Psychiatry*, vol 28, June 1973.

Pfeffer, C.R., "Self-Destructive Behavior in Children and Adolescents." *Psychiatric Clinics of North America*, 8(2), 1981.

Pfeffer, C.R., Plutchik, R., Mizruchi, M.S., "Suicidal and Assaultive Behavior in Children: Classification, Measurement, and Interrelations." *Am J Psychiatry*, 140:154–157, 1983.

Pomeroy, J.C. "Periodicity, Pubescence and Psychiatric Disturbance." Undated paper, SUNY at Stony Brook.

Reeves, J.C., et al. "Attention Deficit, Conduct, Oppositional, and Anxiety Disorders in Children: II. Clinical Characteristics." *J Am Acad Child Adolesc Psychiatry*, 26(2):144–55. 1987.

Rifkin, A., et al. "Psychotropic Medication in Adolescents: A Review." *J Clin Psychiatry*, 47:400–408, 1986.

Rohrkemper, M. "Individual Differences in Students' Perceptions of Routine Classroom Events." *Journal of Educational Psychology*, 77:29, 1985.

Ryan, N.D., Puig-Antich, J. "Pharmacological Treatment of Adolescent Psychiatric Disorders." *Journal of Adolescent Health Care*, 8:137–141, 1987.

Safer, D.J., Allen, R.P. "Stimulant Drug Treatment of Hyperactive Adolescents." *Diseases of the Nervous System*, 36:454–467, 1975.

Satterfield, J.H., et al. "A Prospective Study of Delinquency in 110 Adolescent Boys with Attention Deficit Disorder and 88 Normal Adolescent Boys." *Am J Psychiatry*, 139:6, 1982.

Schools Council (of Britain). "Children and Plastics." London: Macdonald Educational, 1974.

Shaffer, D. "Suicide in Childhood and Early Adolescence." *J Child Psychol Psychiat*, 15:275–291, 1974.

Stewart, M.A. "Disturbance in School." *The Clinical Guide to Child Psychiatry*. Edited by Shaffer, D., et al. New York: The Free Press, 1985.

Taylor, J.F. *The Hyperactive Child and the Family.* New York: Dodd, Mead, 1980.

Trelease, J. *The Read-Aloud Handbook.* New York: Penguin Books, 1982.

Weiss, G., et al. "Hyperactives as Young Adults: A Controlled Prospective Ten-Year Follow-Up of 75 Children." *Arch Gen Psychiatry*, 36:675–681, 1979.

Weiss, G., et al. "Psychiatric Status of Hyperactives as Adults: A Controlled Prospective 15-Year Follow-up of 63 Hyperactive Children." *J Amer Acad Child Adolesc Psychiatry*, 24 (2):211– 220, 1985.

Weiss, G., Hechtman, L. "The Hyperactive Child Syndrome." *Science*, 205:1348–1354, 1979.

Weiss, G., Hechtman, L. *Hyperactive Children Grown Up.* New York: Guilford Press, 1986.

Wender, P.H. "Attention-Deficit Hyperactivity Disorder in Adolescents and Adults." *Psychiatric Disorders in Children and Adolescents*. Edited by Garfinkel, B.D., et al. Philadelphia: W.B. Saunders, 1990.

Werry, J.S., Reeves, J.C., Elkind, G.S. "Attention Deficit, Conduct, Oppositional, and Anxiety Disorders in Children: I. A Review of Research on Differentiating Characteristics." *J Amer Acad Child Adolesc Psychiatry*, 26(2):133–43, 1987.

Youngerman, J., Canino, I.A. "Lithium Carbonate Use in Children and Adolescents: A Survey of the Literature." *Arch Gen Psychiatry*, 35:216–224, 1978.

Zametkin, A.J., et al. "Cerebral Glucose Metabolism in Adults with Hyperactivity of Childhood Onset." *New England J of Med*, 323(20):1361–1366, 1990.

Index

A

Aggression, 19
  lithium and, 82
Alcohol, 93, *See also*
  Drinking
Antipsychotic
  medication, 93
Antisocial behavior, 92
Antisocial
  complications, 89
Antisocial disruptive
  disorders
  Conduct Disorder,
  90
  Oppositional

Defiant Disorder,
  90
Anti-social parents
  and effects on
  children, 123
Assessment scales, 28
Athletic ability, 20
Attention-deficit
  Hyperactivity
  Disorder (ADHD),
  11
  and active over
  sedentary labor,
  122
  adults, categories

Attn.-deficit (*cont'd.*)
of, 120–21
causes of, 75
criteria for severity
of, 29
and drug and
alcohol abuse, 123
educating children
with, 67–74
features associated
with, 56
and higher
education, 121
living with, 55–66
long-term effects
of, 122–24
and self esteem, 122
and social
interactions,
121–22
treatment of, 75–85
diagnosis, 28–31

B

Behavior modification,
47–51, 83–84, 91,
111–13
praise and, 49
punishment and,
49–50
Behavioral disorder

lasting nature of, 5
Behavioral handicaps,
3–13
Benzedrine, 76
Bipolar disorder,
95–97
Bipolar patients
treatment of, 110
Brain damage,
minimal, 21
Brats, 18

C

Carbamazepine. *See*
Tegretol
Child
appearance, 26
laboratory tests,
27–28
physical exam,
27–28
signs of mood
disorder, 26
Child's history
birth and
development,
23–24
family psychiatric,
25
home, 25
medical, 24

presentation, 23
school, 24–25
Clonazepam. *See*
   Klonopin
Cocaine, 94
Coercion, 15
Cognitive problem-
   solving skills
   therapy, 112–13
Concentration, 20
Conduct Disorder
   (CD), 10–11, 22,
   31–32
and antisocial
   behavior, 104
and attention
   deficit, 103
evaluation of,
   102–106
impulsiveness and
   aggressiveness
   and, 100
and juvenile
   delinquency, 104
and low self-esteem,
   100
most visible
   symptom of,
   102–103
nature of, 89–91
treatment of,
   107–113
Conduct Disorder or

Attention Deficit,
   91–92
Conduct Disorder or
   Bipolar Disorder,
   95–97
*Conduct Disorder in
   Childhood and
   Adolescence*, 123
Conduct Disorder or
   Depression, 97–98
Conduct Disorder
   medications
desipramine, 109
imipramine, 109
lithium, 110
Mood stabilizers,
   109
Tegretol, 110
tricyclic
   antidepressants
   (TCAs), 109-110
Conduct Disorder or
   Seizure Disorder,
   93–95
Connors Teacher
   Rating Scale, 28
Connors Abbreviated
   Parent Rating
   Scale, 28
Coordination
   problems, 20
Cylert, 58
side effects of, 81

D

Depakote, 110
Depression
   and aggression, 101
   agitated, 30, 96
   individual therapy
      for, 97
   teenage, 101
Desipramine, 81, 109
Developmental
   milestones, 23–24
*Deviant Children
   Grown Up*, 123
Dexamethasome
   suppression test,
   98
Dexedrine, 58, 76, 81
Dextroamphetamine.
   See Dexedrine
Dextroamphetamine
   sulfate. *See*
   Dexedrine
*Diagnostic and
   Statistical Manual
   of Mental
   Disorders*, 22
Dietary modification,
   84
Disruptive disorders
   age of appearance
      of, 9
   and control of
      actions, 9
   and social
      responsibility,
      9–11
   and society, 6–8
   treatment of, 11–13
   warning signs of,
      14–20
Dosages, 77
Douglas, Virginia, 83
Drinking, 92. *See also*
   Alcohol
Dyslexia, 25

E

Education problems,
   111
Electrocardiogram
   (ECG), 28
   and TCAs, 81
Electroconvulsive
   therapy (ECT),
   93, 96
Electroencephalogram
   (EEG), 28, 94
Electroshock therapy.
   See
   Electroconvulsive
   therapy
Epilepsy, 106

F

Grown Up, 118

Family
  damage within, 111
  relationships, 15–16
  therapy, 97, 112
Family problems
  blaming one
    another, 37
  despair, 38
  emotion, 38
  families at risk, 38
  impulse to harm
    child, 37
  obsession, 37–38
  sibling discontent,
    38
  unreasonable
    expectations, 37
Feingold, Benjamin,
  84
Feingold diet, 84

H

Hallucinogenic drugs
  (PCP and LSD),
  93
Hechtman, Lily T.,
  118
Himmelhoch, J., 94
Homework, 40
Hyperactive Children

I

Imipramine, 68, 109
Immaturity
  as indicator of
    disruptive
    disorder, 7, 18
Impulsivity, 65
Inattention, 65
Individual treatment,
  41

J

John's story, 57–58
Judgment
  between impulse
    and action, 8
Juvenile delinquency
  alternate diagnosis
    of, 105–106

K

Kazdin, Alan E.,
  123–24
Kindling, theory of,
  94
Klonopin, 110

L

Learning one-on-one
hands-on art, 73
hands-on math, 73
physical skills, 73
reading together,
72–73
science collections,
72
social skills, 73–74
Lewis, Dorothy O.,
105
Lithium, 82, 93, 96
Love
as reward, 49

M

Magnesium pemoline.
See Cylert
Marla's story, 68–69
Medication, 12–13
children and, 45–46
combined, 44
as a distraction, 42
drug rebound, 44
drug vacations, 44
effects of years of,
119
general principles
of, 45–46
initiation, 43–44
as an insult, 42
as an interference,
43
maintenance, 44
parents and, 45
prescription, 43
tolerance for, 44
resuming
maintenance, 45
Mellaril. See
Thioridazine
Methylphenidate. See
Ritalin
Mood disorder
lithium and, 82
Moods, 18
Movement problem
and Ritalin, 78

N

Neuroleptics
side effects of, 82
No spanking rule, 37
Nonacademic
activities, 68
Nortriptyline, 98

O

One-on-one relations,
64

Oppositional Defiant
Disorder (ODD),
22, 30–31, 90

P

Paranoid symptoms,
106
Parent management
training, 112
Parenting
change in methods,
63
Ozzie-and-Harriet
form of, 36
Parents
guilt-ridden, 4
Peer relationships, 17
Pharmacological
hypomania, 96
Prevention techniques,
98–100
Primary Mental
Health Project
(PMHP), 41, 99
Promiscuity, 90
Propranolol, 111
Psychiatric evaluation,
21–24
Psychiatric
medications
questions about,
46–47
Psychopharmacology,
76
Psychosis, drug-
related, 78
Psychostimulants, 43,
58
Psychotherapy, 83
Punishment, 63
teaching value of,
49–50

R

Rebelliousness, 65
Reinforcement, 63
Responsibility
development of,
9–11
Reward, 48–49
Ritalin, 58, 59, 60,
65, 68, 76
and home
environment, 80
popularity of, 78
side effects of, 78
Robins, L.N., 123
Rules of games and
Attention-deficit
Hyperactivity
Disorder (ADHD),
56

Rutter, Michael, 106

Suicide, 90, 100–102
Superego, 9

S

School treatment
  establishing contact,
    39–40
  providing structure,
    40
  special programs,
    40–41
  special schools, 39
Schoolwork, 16
Second grade
  hyperactive children
    in, 64
Seizure disorder, 28
Self-esteem, 18–19
Social skills
  absence of, 111
Specialized schools,
  68
Spoiled, 18
Star charts, 83
Steven's story, 58–61
Stimulants, 76
Stop, look, and listen
  method, 83
Substance abusing
  parents and
  effects on
  children, 123

T

Tegretol, 94, 96, 110
Television and video
  games and
  hyperactive
  children, 15
Temporal lobe
  syndrome, 94
Temporal-lobe
  epilepsy, 110
Therapy
  family, 83
  individual, 82–83.
    See also
    Treatment
Thioridazine, 82
Thyroid abnormality,
  27
Tic disorder and
  Ritalin, 78
Timeout system, 50
Tourette's syndrome
  and Ritalin, 78
Treatment of
  disruptive
  disorders
  family treatment,
    36–39

individual
  treatment, 41
medication and
  modification,
  41–51
plan of, 35–36
school treatment,
  39–41
Tricyclic
  antidepressant, 98
Tricyclic
  Antidepressants

(TCAs), 81,
  109–110

V

Valproic acid. *See*
  Depakote

W

Weiss, Gabriella, 118

ABOUT THE AUTHORS

ROSALIE GREENBERG, M.D., is Director of the Child and Adolescent Outpatient Services at Fair Oaks Hospital, Summit, N.J. Dr. Greenberg received her medical degree from Columbia University, where she completed her psychiatric residency. Following her residency, Dr. Greenberg was a Fellow in Child and Adolescent Psychiatry at Columbia. She served as chief resident in child psychiatry and was a recipient of the Edward J. Sachar Award for Clinical Excellence in Child Psychiatry. She is the former Deputy Director of the Pediatric Psychiatry Outpatient Clinic at Columbia, and is an Instructor in Clinical Psychiatry at Columbia University College of Physicians and Surgeons.

LYNNE W. WEISBERG, M.D., Ph.D., is Associate Director of Child and Adolescent Outpatient Services at Fair Oaks Hospital. A Who's Who in American Women, Dr. Weisberg received her Ph.D. from the University of Michigan and her M.D. from the State University of New York. Following her residency at Mount Sinai Hospital, she was a Fellow in Child and Adolescent Psychiatry at Columbia University. Her clinical and teaching interests include the pharmacology of ADHD, aggressive and depressive disorders, as well as the residential treatment of children and adolescents.

Bantam
On Psychology

☐ 28037-6 **MEN WHO HATE WOMEN &
THE WOMEN WHO LOVE THEM**
Dr. Susan Forward $5.99

☐ 26401-X **MORE HOPE AND HELP FOR YOUR NERVES**
Claire Weekes $4.50

☐ 27043-5 **THE POWER OF THE SUBCONSCIOUS MIND**
Dr. J. Murphy $4.50

☐ 34367-X **TEACH ONLY LOVE** Gerald Jampolsky, M.D.
(A Large Format Book) $8.95

ALSO AVAILABLE ON AUDIO CASSETTE

☐ 45142-1 **WHEN AM I GOING TO BE HAPPY? BREAK THE
EMOTIONAL BAD HABITS THAT KEEP YOU FROM
REACHING YOUR POTENTIAL**
Penelope Russianoff, Ph.D $8.95

☐ 45167-7 **TEACH ONLY LOVE** Gerald Jampolsky $8.95

☐ 45218-5 **LIFE IS UNCERTAIN, EAT DESSERT FIRST: Finding
the Joy You Deserve**
Sol Gordon and Harold Brecher $8.95